Come Rain
or
Come Shine

Come Rain
or
Come Shine

FRIENDSHIPS BETWEEN WOMEN

Linda Bucklin

&

Mary Keil

ADAMS MEDIA CORPORATION
Holbrook, Massachusetts

Published by Adams Media Corporation
260 Center Street, Holbrook, MA 02343

ISBN: 1-58062-211-9

Printed in Canada

J I H G F E D C B

Library of Congress Cataloging-in-Publication Data
Bucklin, Linda
Come rain or come shine: friendships between women /
by Linda Bucklin and Mary Keil.
p.   cm.
ISBN 1-58062-211-9
1. Women—Psychology. 2. Female friendship. I. Keil, Mary. II. Title.
HQ1206.B8   1999
302.3'4'082—dc21   99-15773
CIP

This publication is designed to provide accurate and authoritative information with
regard to the subject matter covered. It is sold with the understanding that the publisher
is not engaged in rendering legal, accounting, or other professional advice. If legal advice
or other expert assistance is required, the services of a competent professional person
should be sought.
— From a *Declaration of Principles* jointly adopted by a Committee of the American
Bar Association and a Committee of Publishers and Associations

This book is available at quantity discounts for bulk purchases.
For information, call 1-800-872-5627 (in Massachusetts, 781-767-8100).

Visit our home page at http://www.adamsmedia.com

To my husband, Bill; to Christian and Kris, John and Nick; to all those slender threads of friendship that so enrich our lives.

—LB

To sisters Sally and Jane; my mother, Catherine; Swift, Parker, Joan, John, Val, and Gina; and many other past and current friends who teach me every day.

—MK

Contents

Foreword

*L*oneliness is the great and secret wound of our highly technological culture. As a culture we submit our pain and our problems to experts to be solved. But loneliness cannot be fixed by experts; it is not a wound of the body, it is a wound of the heart. Expertise can't heal loneliness, only friendship can.

Women have healed each other's loneliness since the beginning. The friendship between women goes far deeper than mere companionship, beyond the offering of advice on clothes and makeup or the sharing of recipes. In their friendships women have the capacity to validate and strengthen the life in one another. Women's friendships heal.

Women respond to each other's pain with listening. By wanting to know and letting it matter. By trusting the life in one another. By offering, with their simple attention, a place of acceptance and trust of natural process where even the deepest pain can heal. In their friendships, women do not "fix" one another. They do not see each other as broken. They offer each other sanctuary.

Not all women are good friends; there are those who are competitive, those who undermine, those who are consumed with envy and jealousy, those who manipulate and use. But there is a potential in the friendships between women that exists nowhere else. At its best the friendship between women is transparent to the deep feminine with its profound trust of growth and life. This same archetype is the foundation of all other healing relationships as well.

Some time ago, I invited a class of medical students to consider the way in which they wanted to respond to the vulnerability of their future patients and to write a poem or a prayer about it. One student wrote the following to the patients he would someday have and captured the very essence of relationships that heal.

> *May you find in me the Mother of the World*
> *May my hands be a mother's hands,*
> *My heart be a mother's heart.*
> *May my response to your suffering be a mother's response*
> *to your suffering.*
> *May I sit with you in the dark*
> *as a mother sits in the dark.*
> *May you know through our relationship*
> *that there is something in this world that can be trusted.*

At best, the friendships between women can be like this.

Facing pain alone makes us vulnerable to despair and causes unnecessary suffering. Yet many people face their pain alone because they are unable to reach out and trust others with their vulnerability. People like Jessie.

When Jessie was a new patient, she came into my office a week after missing an appointment and told me that, at the time she was supposed to be here the week before, she had been in the emergency room of our local hospital. I had not known this, and I asked her what had happened. She told me that she had suffered a temporary blockage of her intestine from scarring caused by the radiation used to treat her cancer long ago. The pain had been severe and had lasted for a day, but now it was over.

When the pain began, she had known immediately that it was something of significance. She had packed a small bag, taking her makeup, a nightie, and a mystery she was in the middle of reading. Then she had driven herself twenty-five miles to the hospital.

Having had several intestinal blockages myself, I knew how severe such pain could be. I asked her how she had managed to overcome it and drive. She told me the worst of the pain was intermittent. She had driven until she could not drive any more, then she had pulled off the road and waited for the pain to pass. Sometimes this would taken as long as ten or fifteen minutes. She had thought to bring a pot and a towel with her, and once or twice she had even vomited. She had been very sick, but she had gotten to the hospital. It had taken a long time. Surprised, I asked her why she had not called a friend. She told me it was the middle of the day and everyone was working.

She had spent the next day in the emergency room alone. I asked her why she hadn't called anyone even then. "Why would I call anyone?" she had responded with irritation. "None of my friends know a thing about intestinal obstruction."

"Then why didn't you call me?"

"Well, it's not really your field either," she replied.

"Jessie," I said, "even children instinctively run to others when they fall down."

With a great deal of heat she replied, "Yes, I've never understood that. It's so silly. Kissing the boo-boo doesn't help the pain at all."

I was stunned. "Jessie," I said, "it doesn't help the pain, it helps the loneliness."

Many people deal with their pain as Jessie did. When Jessie was in pain the only thing of value that another person could offer her was expertise. Her mother had died when she was born. It had never occurred to her that anything could be done about the loneliness.

Friendships between women can be a place of refuge from loneliness and indifference, a place where we can know we matter as we are. Such friendships can bless the life in us and strengthen us to deal with whatever we must face elsewhere.

—RACHEL NAOMI REMEN, M.D.
AUTHOR, KITCHEN TABLE WISDOM

Introduction

*F*riendship between women can be a grace-filled gift that can last through the years. Or, at other, hopefully much rarer times, it can be a cross to bear and a lesson to be learned. When I think back over the years of my life, it is measured by the grand sweep of abiding friendships with other females. As a lonely, shy seventh grader badly in need of friends in a new school, I had my world come alive when I received an invitation to a pajama party from the leader of the "city kids," who befriended me. In high school, I had a sidekick who went to activities with me as we, together, explored the new and strange world of the opposite sex. In college I had a "little sister" in my sorority who shared the challenge, joy, and perplexity of young adulthood as we guided each other through thick and thin. During the richest times and the most desperate times comes a woman friend reaching out with patience, humor, and sometimes pain. These kinds of encounters open a new world and allow us to navigate the narrow passage into the next stage of our lives.

There is something easy, something flowing, something sacred that can go on between women. Quickly, communication becomes shorthand, and trust builds through humor and the sharing of those thousands of little experiences that don't count for anything except—in retrospect—simply living life. It may be because we share the same body structure and partake of the knowledge and mystery of creating new life. It may be because we have been misunderstood by the "powers that be" over the centuries and have, at times, had to huddle together to keep body and soul fluid and surviving. Whatever the ingredients, there is an alchemical exchange between certain women that furthers both along the path of life. Linda Bucklin and Mary Keil have modeled this in their work together. They are close friends, and out of that friendship comes this book: *Come Rain or Come Shine: Friendships Between Women.*

This book is a compilation of stories about women connecting to one another. Friendship does not happen between all women. And this is what makes it special, as these wonderful stories so clearly teach us. Sometimes the circumstances of life—like moving to a new city, or losing your job, or entering your child in school—create a clear opportunity. But rarely does it happen automatically. Openness to friendship is a key ingredient even though recognition of a woman as a friend may not happen for quite some time. Many times the friendship has to go through some crisis or trial, some event that forges a bond and solidifies trust.

Inevitably, the themes of difficulty and betrayal are woven into these stories, for the authors wisely know that friendship between women must be tested in the cold winds of the shadow that we all carry. Seeing another woman deeply and clearly and understanding her motivations are part of friendship.

Sometimes it takes painful and disappointing experiences to begin to value ourselves as friends. Some of us need to learn that what we offer in friendship is rich and is worth its weight in gold. We must learn discernment about when to offer it and when it must be withdrawn because the other is not able to appreciate the potential gift of friendship.

These short, compact stories are meant to be savored and reflected upon. They can be read slowly over lazy days or used as a morning reflection before running off to work. What they offer is a small and clear window into the female heart.

—THE REVEREND DR. LAUREN ARTRESS
CANON FOR SPECIAL MINISTRIES
GRACE CATHEDRAL, SAN FRANCISCO
AUTHOR, *WALKING THE SACRED PATH:*
REDISCOVERING THE LABYRINTH AS A SACRED TOOL

Fearing Paris

Suppose that what you fear
could be trapped
and held in Paris.
Then you would have
the courage to go
everywhere in the world.
All the directions of the compass
open to you,
except the degrees east or west
of true north
that lead to Paris.
Still, you wouldn't dare
put your toes
smack dab on the city limit line.
You're not really willing
to stand on a mountainside
miles away,
and watch the Paris lights
come up at night.
Just to be on the safe side,
you decide to stay completely
out of France.
But then danger
seems too close
even to those boundaries,
and you feel
the timid part of you
covering the whole globe again.
You need the kind of friend
who learns your secret and says,
"See Paris first."

—M. Truman Cooper

ONE

~

Within the Family–Where Friendship Begins

*W*here does friendship begin? Since our families are where we form our first significant bonds, this is where we are initially exposed to the ways people who supposedly care about each other interact. This is where we learn early relationship lessons that influence us in our friendships as we grow up.

Those of us who are fortunate enough to see and experience loving, trusting, truthful relationships in our original families learn good lessons right from the start. Given those solid examples, we are then well equipped to recreate healthy friendships in the outside world.

Susan and Molly, sisters three years apart, have been best friends their whole lives. Growing up with a critical and competitive mother, they turned to each other for support. With Molly, Susan felt safe and free to share her innermost thoughts because she knew she wouldn't be judged or criticized. Molly has also always given Susan the space she needed, as Molly calls it, "to grow an idea," which she, as a creative person, values highly. In return Molly is grateful to Susan for always making her feel important and appreciated. They each understand the give and take in friendship.

~

Carole wasn't close to her mother, but fortunately she had a grandmother she loved. This strong bond enabled

Carole, when divorced and raising her daughter alone, to be a very present and supportive mother, as her grandmother had been to her.

Others of us are not so lucky and may spend years pursuing or being in unfulfilling relationships because that is what we learned as children. It's difficult to recognize that what is most familiar to us may be harmful; it's hard to let go of damaging patterns from childhood. But if we don't, we can easily fall into the trap of forming unhealthy friendships as adults.

Growing up, Joan, the oldest of six children, was too busy with family obligations to have any time or energy left to form friendships outside the family. She had four brothers and a chauvinist father preventing her from having a life of her own. When she went to college and had more freedom, at first Joan found it difficult to form friendships because she'd had no practice. But because of the friends she found, she came to understand the importance of friendship outside the family and has made sure her daughter, now a teenager, has plenty of time to enjoy her friends.

Many women have wonderful friendships within their families. They are well aware of the joy that these good, loving relationships bring. These women also typically enjoy successful friendships with nonfamily members.

Amy's mother died when Amy was in her early twenties. Years later, when Amy's son got engaged, Amy gave her future daughter-in-law a strand of pearls that had belonged to her mother. Chris was thrilled, and this gift opened her up to start sharing many intimate parts of her life with Amy. Chris's response touched Amy deeply, for she never had the chance as an adult to have moments like that with her own mother. The gift of the pearls linked the three women together and filled up that empty space in Amy's heart.

~

Julie grew up in a small community where her extended family had lived for generations. She was surrounded by loving "family-friends." When she and her husband had to move across the country, Julie initially felt very lonely. Since her own family was so far away, friends took on a greater significance, and she formed friendships she might not have formed had there been family around to fill the void. Friends became her substitute family, and, taking cues from her childhood, she organized family picnics, birthday celebrations, and even holiday meals with her new friends.

Others reflect on the sadness they feel being alienated from their families and mention issues with friends that seem to mirror the problems they had within their family. If we are courageous enough to face the pain that our unhappy family relationships caused and to take steps to change our ways of relating, we gain greater self-awareness. We are then free to enjoy healthy, fulfilling friendships.

Family Comes First

I am Chinese-American. My father came here in 1952, when he was twenty-one, started with nothing, and became very successful. He met my mother through a matchmaker and brought her back from Hong Kong. It was a love match, and they still hold hands. I am the oldest of six children. My mother had a child every year for five years and then one more five years later. I have lived in San Francisco my whole life. My father had a successful contracting career and both parents are still actively involved in the city.

This is about my great friendship with my mother—the "glue" in our large, close-knit family. The real turning point in our relationship came when I was about eleven or twelve. I remember this so distinctly. The family was having dinner, and, as usual, everyone was talking away to each other—in English. I looked over at my mom. No one was talking to her, and she was sitting there not saying a word and looking withdrawn and sad. For some reason, at that very moment, I really saw her. I saw how unhappy she was. I saw how left out she felt, partly because of language and partly because we were all absorbed in our own lives. I saw how she did everything for us and that, for her, the family always came first. I saw how selfishly we used her. I saw what her life must be like, always at home, with only her weekly mahjong game as her own time. Not only did she put the family first but, in addition, at that time, my father brought over from China quite a few relatives to settle here, and we frequently had others living in our house with us for up to two years while they got established here. My mother cared for and fed them, too. My heart opened to her in that moment of recognition.

As the eldest, I held a lot of influence with my siblings, and I had a talk with my three sisters and two brothers. I told them that we had to make an effort to talk to Mom and to include her, somehow to try to make her happy. I told them we were all being selfish and into ourselves, without any regard for her. I guess they listened to me, but I heard myself the loudest.

I think from then on I made it a point to be close to my mom, and that close relationship continues to this day. She makes sure we stay a very tight family. Five out of the six of us live here still, and twice a week we all go over to our parents' house, no matter what. But I am the closest to our mother, and I believe that started back then when I really saw her.

I don't have someone I would call my best friend, but my mother is certainly right up there. She is truly there for me emotionally, mentally, physically, even financially. Every morning around 6 or 6:30, after she does tai chi, she comes over to my house, feeds my four children a hot breakfast, helps them get dressed and ready for school, and makes them a hot lunch. She has been doing this for eight years and misses only when she is away on one of the many cruises she and my father take with their large group of friends. I can't even say how much this means to me.

A few years ago, I lost a baby. I was in the middle of a big project at my son's school and had been up late working on it. She came over immediately to be with me. She took over caring for the kids. She made me get in bed. She fed me and even massaged my toes. It was a very sad time for me, and I know she felt my sadness as I did.

Once, I was telling her about some problems my husband and I were having with our business. I was worried about our being able to pay some bills. A few hours later, my father called and asked me if we needed a loan. I wouldn't have been able to ask my father directly for help, and I hadn't been asking her either, but she took it upon herself to talk to my dad.

Yes, my mother is the glue in our family, and her love is a bedrock for me. Every day she shows her love for me and every member of our family. She has passed her firm belief that family is first on to me. I live for my family, and I know I got that passion and loyalty from her.

—SHARON, 35, SAN FRANCISCO

Comment:
When we have healthy, loving parenting examples in our family of origin, it is natural to pass this legacy on to the next generation.

Friendship Lessons from Childhood

While we are continually learning lessons of friendship throughout our lives from friends and from our experiences in the world, I believe we receive our first ones within our family of origin. It is here we are exposed to ways of relating that we will carry on into relationships outside this original circle. It is here we learn the patterns of behavior that we recreate in our later friendships.

If we are lucky, we learn about trust, about being seen and loved for who we are. We learn about the value of true connections. We begin to understand what it means and how it feels to be treated fairly and well; as a result we are much more likely to form nurturing, strong friendships as adults. If we are unlucky, we are exposed to unhealthy relationships, early examples that serve to influence adversely how we act in our friendships later on.

For the first six years of my life, my nurse, Frances, was my surrogate mother and father. I really don't have many memories of my parents before she left except vague impressions—a soft fragrance left by my mother after she had said goodnight; a loud, teasing voice followed by heavy footsteps that were my father's; combined laughter and the smell of cigarette smoke that surrounded them both.

What I do remember, though, is the strong, centered presence of Frances in my life. I remember her reading to me, holding me and rocking me, singing songs to me. I know that when I looked at her, she smiled and listened closely to what I said, then nodded wisely. She tied ribbons in my hair. She protected me and stood up for me. She was honest and consistent and provided a safe place for me to be vulnerable and true to myself; she taught me about trust. Through her loving me kindly and well, I learned how important kindness and trust are between friends.

After Frances left, I turned to my mother for emotional sustenance, and here the lessons I learned about friendship become more complicated. Whereas Frances and I had been an island unto ourselves, I became entangled in a web of relationships that had barely existed for me. They would influence my choice and quality of friendships, though fortunately the legacy of Frances's love and my mother's kindness prevailed long-term.

My mother was gentle, spiritual, and creative, and I know that I am attracted to women who have these qualities. But she wasn't strong or confident enough to carry me and be the consistent, loyal mother that Frances had been, and so her ambivalence countered the strength of Frances's influence, causing complications in how I looked at friendship.

Her keeping me at arm's length was tied up in her relationship to Dad. He demanded absolute loyalty, approving only of bonds within our family that he controlled and that were linked directly to him. My mother had to distance herself from me to placate him. Had she ever dared to strongly declare her love for me, had she "chosen" me just one time, she would have risked his anger, something she was not willing to do.

Because my mother needed to be safe above all else, she put my father first in her life. She loved him and did everything she could to please him, not realizing that it wouldn't matter to him, that no matter how hard she tried, ultimately she would be unable to reach him. From her I received two messages: that it was too dangerous in our family for her to reveal our deep connection and that it was O.K. to give up her power to Dad. Thus she disowned me and disowned her true self as well.

As an adult I made friends with women with whom I could unknowingly replay the scenario I'd learned from my parents. I chose friends who, like my mother, were elusive or even disowning, who had to keep their feelings and their true selves hidden, and who were afraid to celebrate our friendship. Or I would have friends who, like my father, played the abusive power game, and I, in turn, would acquiesce and give up my power to them, just as my mother had done with my father. Either way, I was not being true to myself.

Fortunately, I still carried with me the memory of Frances's friendship, thus providing me with a healthy reference point. I wanted my friends to act as Frances had acted toward me—in a straightforward, consistent, loving way. I wanted them to be either stronger and more loving with me (as I wished my mother had been with me) or less manipulative and less abusive of me (as I wished my father had been with me). Again and again I would try to change them, willing them to be more real and more accountable. But when challenged, most of these friends would either walk away or behave in a punitive manner toward me.

While in therapy I became conscious of all the baggage I was carrying. I saw my shortcomings, and I also faced up to the disappointment and pain I was feeling from certain of my friendships. I began to see more clearly the impact that my early lessons of friendship, ones that Frances and my parents taught me, were having on my current friendships. I saw which of my friendships were healthy and working and which were the ones I needed to step away from. I also saw how I could become a better friend.

Not only have these childhood lessons shown me in very different ways just how necessary it is to be authentic and true to myself, they have also helped me find friendship on a clear and deep level. In thinking about friendship, I always come back to my nurse, Frances. I have never forgotten her example of standing up to my father and challenging him when she felt he was out of line or too much of a bully. I realize now how courageous she was and how true she stayed to her inner core, two qualities essential in healthy friendship. After all, she was in my father's employ—her living depended on him—and a more cowardly (and less integrated) person might have kept silent.

But she was my champion. I knew I could count on her not only to protect me but also to speak up for me when I needed her to. I don't remember a specific incident leading up to Frances's leaving, but a month before my younger brother was born, Dad fired her. Knowing how devastated I would be should I realize she was gone for good, my mother led me to believe that Frances was on vacation and would return at some indefinite date. The more I asked, the more vague my mother's answers became. When Miss Cooke, a stern English governess, arrived to care for my brother, I knew without a doubt that Frances would never be coming back.

One weekend soon thereafter, I went up to the ranch with my parents. I remember going on a hike with my father, the very same hike that had been a favorite with Frances and me.

Since I had last been there, the foreman had grazed his cattle in those fields, and so I had my first glimpse of cow pies, which immediately intrigued me. I found I could use them as stepping stones, and quickly I made up a game of jumping from one to the next without touching the dry grass beneath.

What I didn't know and what my father did was that they weren't all dried out, that some were a lot fresher than others. He told me later that he just couldn't wait for me to land on one that was soft. I did, finally, and of course I slipped and got cow manure all over me, on my jeans, my hands, in my face and hair. I sat stunned for a minute and then burst into tears. My father laughed, saying, "How could anyone be so stupid?"

Suddenly I felt Frances nearby and even turned around to see if she had by some miracle come home to me. There was no one by my side, but I remember clearly to this day the feeling I had of her presence. I turned to Dad and said in a loud voice, "How can you be so mean to such a beautiful little girl?" He didn't answer, and then I got up, and we walked back to the house in silence. I later heard him telling my mother how spoiled I had become because of Frances and that it was a good thing he had fired her.

While I must admit there have been times, some very dark times, when I almost forgot the sound of Frances's voice and the feel of her strong body next to mine, I never gave in to Dad the way the rest of my family did. Because Frances was my witness and defended me, I finally managed to stand up for myself and step away with my soul intact. Her example has led me to choose close friends who are courageous and act as Frances did with me. I, in turn, try to be there in the same way with them. Her loving friendship is forever imprinted on my heart.

—LB

Aunt Ruth

I have had quite a few very important pen pals in my life. In fact, to me "pen pal" is synonymous with trusted, intimate friend. From about the age of ten on, I carried on a regular correspondence with my Aunt Ruth, my father's second oldest sister. I don't remember how it got started, but we wrote to each other regularly, back and forth between Santa Fe, where she lived with her husband and my three girl cousins, and the various places I lived growing up. The letters became less and less frequent once I went away to college, but by then their value had been well proven in my life.

I don't remember specifically what I said to her. I probably told her what was going on in my life, but I do remember how much I looked forward both to writing to her and to reading her responses. She wrote as she spoke, rapidly and conversation-ally, usually typing and totally ignoring her typos. I enjoyed reading her family's news, but best of all, she always commented on some accomplishment I had mentioned in my last letter in a way that made me feel proud, appreciated, and special. The pen pal relationship we had was all mine, and that seemed important to me as the middle one of three sisters. She, by the way, had been the middle child of her family of five, and, while I've never asked her if she "chose" me because of that, I like to think she knew we middles need some special treatment sometimes. She didn't try to be a parent to me but I was aware she was family. My special fondness for her continues to this day as she approaches ninety.

Once, years later, when I told her how much I had appreciated our correspondence, she told me that she continued the tradition we started and had both a granddaughter and a grandniece as pen pals after me.

Since she wrote just as she spoke—simply, clearly, and with great enthusiasm—her authenticity in writing inspired me to form, hear, and trust my own voice, received so lovingly as it was by her. In fact, I believe that the writer I am today and the love I have for the written word—particularly letters—began so many years ago with our correspondence. I keep in my heart always her unconditional acceptance of me as expressed within all those Santa Fe–postmarked envelopes over the years.

—MK

Letting Laird Go

My daughter, Laird, in her late twenties, and I have always
been very close friends. She was studying to be an actress and
had moved to Los Angeles. I missed having her nearby but
knew that she'd made the right decision for her career. Soon
after she'd settled in, she met a man and fell in love. I didn't
know anything about him or his family; what I did glean over
the ensuing months from Laird—he was older, from a vastly
different background, and a struggling actor with an uncertain
future—made me feel very uneasy about any sort of long-term
relationship.

My husband and I decided that the best way to handle this
situation was to get to know him better. He came with us on
several family trips, yet afterward, we still didn't feel comfortable around him; he didn't really fit into our family picture,
and I felt he was affecting my friendship with Laird. I
expressed my deep concerns to her, who, to her credit, always

listened nondefensively. I kept my focus on what was most important to me—which was to keep a good relationship with my daughter.

Recently, Laird told me that she was moving into John's house. She wanted me to come visit, help with decorating , and go with her to John's acting class. I happily flew to meet her for the weekend. When I walked into his house, I was struck by how comfortable and nice it was. Laird led me to their bedroom and said that she and I would be sleeping there; John would be on the couch downstairs. Together we went to Laird's two auditions, and that evening the three of us drove over to a theater where John taught acting. I sat down in the dark room and watched my daughter as she climbed onto the stage.

Over the next five hours I observed John in his element. He was intense and completely absorbed in what he was doing, and his talents and passion for the theater, for teaching and directing, were obvious. It was a delight to see him on his own turf, doing what he loved and excelled in. I was also amazed at what he brought out in Laird onstage. I recognized the authenticity and strength of his creative spirit, and suddenly I really understood who he was. At that moment he came alive for me, and I accepted what he and my daughter had together.

When we got home that night, the three of us stayed up talking and discussing what had gone on, and then Laird and I went to bed. When we turned out the lights, I remember feeling so happy that I was sharing that big double bed with my daughter. Never would I have been able to experience this same closeness with my own mother; in fact, I reminded myself, I wouldn't have even wanted her to come watch me rehearse for anything. I went to sleep knowing that what was most important to me was to cherish my friendship with my daughter.

The next day Laird had appointments, and so I found myself at the breakfast table alone with John. Three hours later we were still talking, and I almost missed my plane back home. I wrote Laird a letter saying that I loved getting to know John, and that I could better understand now why she had chosen him. I told her that I trusted her judgment. I made it clear that whatever choices she wanted to make, I would always support her and love her. After I'd mailed it, a great sense of peace came over me.

Laird called soon thereafter to say how much she appreciated my letter. She told me she'd read it to John, and that they'd both cried. All this made me realize that when I stopped trying to control my daughter and let go of my expectations, our relationship shifted dramatically. We could again experience the closeness we'd had before John. I understood that it is my daughter's life to live, not mine, and that I could finally set her free, enabling our friendship to get back on track.

—ANNE, 54, SAN FRANCISCO

Comment:

When a mother and daughter are great friends, there comes a time when the mother has to cease exercising parental control and let the daughter choose her own way. Real friendship involves accepting a friend for who she is—in and out of a family.

The Gift of Acceptance

My mother died recently, and although I still miss her very much, she gave me a gift before she died that I can now carry with me and hope to pass on to my daughters.

As a mother she was always very formal and remote; she did not know how to share intimate feelings with me. When I was fifteen she just left our home one day and didn't return for two months. Not a word of explanation. No one, not even my father, mentioned the fact that she was gone. In our family, we just didn't talk.

It wasn't until I was married, had had two daughters, and was heading for a severe depression that I turned to my mother and asked her why she'd left. I needed to know more of her story so I could make some sense of why I was so unhappy.

She told me she'd been very unhappy in her marriage and had wanted to get out of it but then didn't. "Nobody in those days got a divorce," she said. Finally, I learned the reason why she had disappeared for two months so long ago.

In the process of her opening up to me, she ventured out of her very private shell and shared with me many of her feelings of pain and loss. It was at this moment that we broke a long-standing pattern in our family—that of not speaking. This extraordinary conversation marked the turning point in our relationship, and we began our journey of reconciliation.

This reconciliation allowed me to understand much more about myself and my needs. Consequently, I was better able to leave a long, lonely marriage. I later get together with a childhood sweetheart. I thought my mother might disapprove, but instead she flew out to be with us at Thanksgiving. At the dinner table she looked around at my new husband and me and our respective kids, raised her glass, and toasted us. We all felt her blessing.

Eleven days after this Thanksgiving gift of acceptance, she died unexpectedly. While I mourn her death, I celebrate the completeness of our relationship. Finally we understood each other. I accepted the absence of an intimate mother in my growing-up years, and she accepted my decision to do something she hadn't had the courage to do. Having this late shift in my mother's and my relationship makes me appreciate the friendship I enjoy with my own daughters.

—SHEILA, 53, SPOKANE, WA

Comment:
When a parent acknowledges her own story to her child, this opens up many doors for acceptance and reconciliation between them.

What Mom Never Told Me

It wasn't until my mother's funeral that I had any idea how important her women friends were to her. On that sad day, four women I had known since childhood in our small Texas town tearfully said my mother had been one of their closest friends.

Each one told me my mother had made a big difference in her life. While it warmed my grieving heart to know that others would miss her as I would, I felt confused because my mother had never told me where friendship fit in her life. In fact, I grew up receiving the message from her that men were the ones who mattered and that women friends would and should always take a back seat to the men in your life.

I never witnessed the shared confidences over coffee at the kitchen table, for example. I never saw my mother drop her domestic duties to go to the aid of a friend or even go out alone with a friend. My father and she did everything together. She put him first, always. Consequently, it wasn't until my early thirties that I made my first real woman friend, and that was because she pursued me. I had patterned my life after my mother's and had always put men first.

When I got divorced, a woman at work, also recently divorced, asked me if I wanted to go to the movies with her. The invitation took me aback because I'd had no experience enjoying even the simplest activity with another woman. I initially even thought the woman was coming on to me. Now my women friends are an indispensable part of my life. They are there for me, as I am there for them.

While I wish I could talk to my mother about her friendships with the women at her funeral, I understand she was following her generation's norm of a woman's putting the men in her life ahead of women. I wish she had taught me as a child to value women more, but I am very glad I at least learned it as an adult. And it heartens me to know, even if she didn't tell me,

that she actually did share my newfound belief in the importance of having good friends.

—JUDY, 48, SUMMIT, NJ

Comment:
Even after a parent has died, we are comforted to know
that we shared similar values—including the impor-
tance of good women friends.

The Library

When Mom died years ago, Dad made it clear that he no longer
wanted to speak or hear her name. It was as if their thirty-six-year
marriage had never happened. He wiped her life clean off his slate
and expected us, his children, to do the same. While I loved my
mother and missed her terribly, I was afraid to defy my father, and
so I hid her memory and my love for her deep inside me.

In my forties, I became involved in a capital campaign for
my church. As I was looking over the building plans, I suddenly
saw how wonderful it would be if the future library there were
named in memory of my mother. For years I had been wanting
to honor her in a strong, dignified way for all the world to see,
but until that point I hadn't figured out what to do.

Since I was still carrying around a lot of unresolved feelings
surrounding Mom's death, I knew that this would be a difficult
journey for me. Every call to an old friend of hers would bring up
not only the intense pain I felt surrounding her death but also

the fear I still had of ever crossing Dad. But I also understood that here was a very appropriate and obvious way to celebrate my mother's life, and so I decided to go ahead with the project.

Her friends were thrilled to participate in a memorial for her. But one in particular, Mrs. Metcalf, stands out in my mind as representative of the collective love they all had for my mother. I remember the day I went to visit her to ask for her support. During our conversation about contributing to the library, she presented me with a box. When I opened it, I saw four crystal wine glasses. She explained that they were part of a collection given to her by my mother over the years of their friendship, and that she now wanted to start giving them to me in honor of her love for Mom.

She went on to speak of my mother's love of books, art, opera, travel, and new ideas, and especially of her family and friends. She said that of all her friends Mom truly heard the song of life, a song she shared with all those around her. She mentioned my mother's generosity of spirit that touched so many people.

As Mrs. Metcalf was reminiscing, I was swept along in the tide of her memories. I saw myself picking roses with Mom in the garden at the ranch. I saw us riding together, Mom gracefully astride Dune, her white mare. I remembered the soft touch of her hand on mine, and I heard once again her gentle voice calling out to me. It was almost as if she were sitting right there next to us enjoying the love we both felt so strongly for her.

I raised the necessary funds, and now there is a beautiful library named in honor of my mother. More important, my love for my mother, who died before we could complete our friendship as adults, is unencumbered now. When I walk into that room, I am filled with a sense of her presence, and I feel we've come home to each other.

—LB

Comment:
It's never too late to heal a mother-daughter relationship and become friends. Sometimes this happens, with the help of friends, even after the mother has died.

Friends Since the Womb

I am eighty-three and consider myself to be very lucky when it comes to friends. It runs in the family. I have been blessed with a truly lifelong friend—my sister Marge. Four years my senior, she has always told me that she loved me even before I was born because she wanted a little sister so badly. Our family has always been close. My mother and her sister were very close, and my sister and I have continued the tradition. I suppose our mother talked so fondly of her sister that my sister wanted us to have the same kind of relationship they had.

Our mother also taught us to get along. I remember if I complained about someone, my mother would say, "I'm not interested in what you don't like about so-and-so, only what you like." I guess we learned to look at the good in people. The sibling rivalry people talk about just didn't exist between Marge and me. I never felt like I was a nuisance to her. She was always willing to include me and thought everything I did was wonderful. I felt that her love for me and certainly mine for her have never wavered. She's been my strongest supporter throughout my life, there for me whenever I've needed her, and I have been through some difficult times, like losing my only child in an accident at the age of twenty, and losing my husband to Alzheimer's.

I remember one story of how I used to sing "My country 'tis of V" instead of "thee." My mother said she was going to correct me, but my sister said, "Don't tell her; it's so cute." I found a picture recently of Marge and me when we were about eight and four. We have these huge ribbons in our hair. My hand is on Marge's shoulder. That picture represents how we still feel about each other.

As young girls, she lent me her clothes, even though I was sloppier than she was and occasionally returned a sweater with a button missing or a blouse with a spot on it. I was her maid of honor and only attendant at her wedding, and she was my matron of honor and only attendant at my wedding. I remember when I gave my first big party as a newlywed, Marge called and asked, "Do you want me to tell you what needs doing?" It was a genuine question; she didn't presume that I wanted her advice, but, of course, I did. She suggested I serve one unusual dish that would make a real impression. I don't remember what I served, but I know I have continued that tradition to this day.

When World War II came, both of our husbands went away for two and a half years. Her husband was an officer, however, and my husband had been drafted at thirty-three. As we didn't have much money, Marge invited my little son and me to come live with her, her son, and our mother. We had a grand time together, and things worked like magic. One week I would do all the meals and she would clean up; the next week we'd switch. Our sons, who were toddlers at the time, became the best of friends as well and that friendship continued until my son's death.

Both widows now, we spend as much time together as we can, considering that we both love where we live. I spend six weeks of the summer with her up north, either at her house in New Jersey or up on the Cape. Marge spends six weeks with me at my home in Florida. We talk every Saturday on the phone to get caught up on the news of the week. While I find Florida a cheerful place to live, Marge doesn't want to live in Florida. She's lived in the same house for fifty-one years, and that is where she wants to stay. Besides, her two sons and their families live nearby.

We never tire of being together even after all these years. I consider myself to be a very lucky person. I have always been surrounded by super people. For us, despite losses in our lives, growing old hasn't been the lonely time it is often thought of because we have each other.

—LOIS, 83, VENICE, FL

A Houseful of Friends

I grew up in a large Catholic family of seven children in a small town in Iowa. I am very close to all my brothers and sisters. Now spread far and wide geographically, we speak on the phone, write letters, and eagerly look forward to the reunion at my parents' house every summer when as many of us get together as possible. Of course, each relationship I have is different because we are all different. I even admit I have one brother in particular to whom I feel the closest. But I believe that because of the positive experience I had growing up in such a close family, and because my parents gave us equal love and support, I have never had difficulty making friends. I guess I learned that I value having close personal relationships because my relationships with my siblings were, in general, enriching.

When my husband and I were getting to know each other many years ago, I was surprised at how differently he and his brother and sister interacted. There seemed to be a lot of competition, distrust, and just plain meanness. Rich is crazy about my family because we're all such great friends and the kind of tension he feels with his siblings is absent. He looks forward to the reunions as much as I do, as he has established his own relationships with my family. I feel so lucky that the lessons I learned about friendship within my own family have convinced me that there is ever more to give to the people we care about in our lives, whether they are family or not.

—JEAN, 49, LOS ANGELES

Comment:
Fair and equal treatment makes it possible for siblings to be good friends for life and encourages us to create healthy friendships outside the family.

The Power of Parents

I feel sad when I hear a woman talk about how close she is to her sister. My sister, who is six years older, and I are not friends. We never have been. And with her unwillingness to look at why this is so, I doubt we ever will be. My mother's behavior made this friendship impossible.

When I was born, she told everyone in the family and in the outside world that I was her favorite and that she loved me best. Even though our father tried to equal the scales, he couldn't counteract the excessive attention my mother paid to me. Naturally, my sister resented this terribly, and even though my mother has been dead ten years now, the unhealthy dynamics she set up were so powerful that my sister cannot forgive me. Every chance she gets, she still undermines me.

This upsets me, so I've talked with other women who are not friends with their siblings and have learned that my situation isn't unique. My friend Faye grew up with an abusive father who controlled every relationship within the family. He needed to be the center of attention and prevented his children from being friends for fear of losing any of his power.

As an adult she finally found the courage to start talking with her siblings about how unhappy she'd been growing up. She naively thought that once she started insisting on the truth being told they could all be free to interact in healthier ways. How wrong she was.

The moment she started speaking up, her siblings denied that anything painful had ever happened to her or to them, and they rallied around their father, the very person who had mistreated them. There, by his side, they could feel temporarily safe from looking at anything unpleasant from their past. They could also direct his anger away from them and toward Faye. She had to end all contact with her family.

Our experiences have helped me realize now how often a lack of friendship with siblings begins in childhood. Fortunately, I learned this in time to be a better parent to my three children, who are great friends, and I feel lucky to have broken the pattern.

—ANDREA, 43, HOUSTON

My Older Sister

I consider myself very lucky because my lifelong friendship with my older sister has only grown better with each passing year. Although she remembers with regret that she was mean to me when we were very small, what I remember is that I had a big sister I could count on for just about anything. What major event of my life has she not been present for? She is the first person I think of when I want to share a special moment, whether the moment is a happy one or a challenging one. She has truly been there for me endlessly over the years. For instance, my sophomore year of college, my dormitory had a terrible fire, leaving many of us without our possessions. Several days after the fire, half a dozen big boxes stuffed full of clothing arrived. She had collected donations from her dorm mates, never telling me she was doing so.

She has always been a sounding board for me. She is the first person I talked to about my decision to leave my first husband. I would say I went to her for advice all the time. She would say I never took it. But her gift to me was giving me a safe space to talk so that my inner voice could speak out. She was a superb listener. Sometimes I wanted her to tell me what to do because I respected her intelligence and perspective on things so much. But I really wanted to be able to talk something through with her, my most trusted friend, and then reach my own decision or conclusion. She allowed me to do that.

However, as my "big" sister, she felt she had a certain role to fill, and that role led to a certain unevenness in our relationship. While I had no hesitations calling her when I wanted to, I felt she gave far more to me than she allowed me to give to her. After all, a family "rule" was that big sisters don't go to little sisters for help because they are stronger, wiser, and more experienced, etc. Even though our age difference became less and less significant, even though we both had friends the other's age whom we regarded as our equals, we still had that familial role to play out. Truly, I would do anything for her—all she had to do was ask me, but she had trouble doing that. I had to make the offer, then she'd accept.

A few years ago, she mentioned some problems she and her husband were having refinancing their mortgage. The bank told them they had too much high-interest credit card debt. My husband and I had just sold our house and didn't intend to buy again right away, so we were liquid. I asked her point-blank how much she needed to clean up the credit card debt. She named a figure. My husband and I agreed to a loan, prepared a note, and sent it and a check to her. Their new mortgage was approved and we were soon repaid out of the higher proceeds. It felt great to be able to help her like that.

For many years we lived in the same city, but could go for several weeks without speaking. Sometimes I played a game with her. I forced myself not to call her, and then I just waited to see if she would call me. Actually, it was solitaire because she never knew the rules. I figured out that when things weren't going that well, she'd go into a shell. It was hard for her, because of our pattern, to come to me for help.

One day, after quite a long hiatus, I felt compelled to call her. When I asked her how she was, she started crying. She had had a very disturbing sexual experience the night before and was in a lot of pain. I rushed to her apartment. She was obviously very sick, and I knew she needed immediate medical attention. I called our OB-GYN and insisted she see my sister right away. Then I got her dressed, and we took a cab to the doctor, who prescribed a massive antibiotic and made it clear my sister had been only hours away from the ER. I took her back home and put her to bed. Then I went to the drugstore to have the prescription filled, bought some food for her so she wouldn't have to leave the apartment until she felt better, and stayed with her until she felt ready for me to leave.

I was, of course, a grown woman with a responsible career, fully capable of taking charge of this or many other situations. But my being in the driver's seat, so to speak, simply didn't fit our big sister–little sister pattern. To me it was obvious I would and could do anything for her, yet I think she had always felt uncomfortable about taking my help. That day, however, she was at her most vulnerable, and out of that vulnerability, our relationship subtly shifted.

I still feel she has made far more of a difference in my life than I in hers because I have so thoroughly invited her to do so. But I have been there for her at some key points, whether by plan or by accident, and I now believe that she knows, as I do, that we will always be there for each other.

—MK

Not Having Our Say

My mother and her older sister are in their early eighties. Their younger sister has died, and they are alone now. Yet friendship doesn't come easily to these two women because of how my aunt treated my mother many years ago.

The incident involved my aunt's abusing her power over an inheritance by insisting that she was more deserving than my mother to inherit something. She did not see my mother as her equal and therefore did not treat her fairly. As a result, my mother doesn't trust her, nor does she feel loved or accepted by her sister. And the reality may just be that my aunt's emotional needs and my mother's insecurities, as they developed in their family growing up, may make real loving friendship between them impossible.

The dynamic between them may be responsible for my mother's own reticence with her friends. She has always been reluctant to share personal things with her friends. I don't think she feels safe, just as she had reason not to feel safe with her older sister. Since my own relationship with my sister is so strong, I feel sorry for what both of them are missing. I see them stuck in the same patterns that were established many, many decades earlier.

I think I was very inspired by how the Delany sisters depicted their lives in their wonderful joint autobiography, *Having Our Say*, and have fantasized about living with my sister when we are widowed and older. It makes me very sad for my mother and aunt that they are missing out on finishing their lives sharing such a special friendship. Our mother's painful experiences, however, did not prevent my sister and me from having an incredibly loving, trusting relationship, and I am ever more aware what a gift that is.

—KAREN, 48, ROCHESTER, NY

Comment:
It is to be treasured when sisters are close or best friends, and what a loss for both of them when they aren't.

A Sister's Witness

Several years ago, my sister dropped a bombshell on our family that led me into a period of examination as to how our relationship growing up impacted my relationships both with her as an adult and with friends. She told us that, through therapy, she had recovered memories of sexual abuse by our father, who died many years ago. The aftermath has been traumatic, the most difficult outcome being that my sister and mother are no longer in contact.

As difficult as it was, I ended up bearing witness to her story, although there is no doubt her news turned me topsy-turvy as well. I went through periods of doubt, resistance, anger, and concern about repressed memories of my own, even returning to therapy. But I was determined to hear what my sister had to say, both for her sake and because I sensed I could gain a greater understanding of unresolved issues from my childhood, including why I felt so jealous of her when we were growing up.

My journey from resenting her to regarding her as a friend is tied to her experience with our father and my intuitively sensing that something was going on between them. I know he spent special time with her and not with me, which set up a pattern of jealousy which I believe I carried into my friendships, particularly as it related to men. My jealousy of my sister's unspoken but "special" relationship with our father played out in different ways. For example, if a boyfriend showed even the slightest friendly interest in a friend of mine or in a sister, I was very threatened, sure he would "choose" her over me.

Through hard work, my sister is on the road to recovery. I believe that my bearing witness to her story and doing my own inner work have enabled us to become the friends we never were growing up.

—SAMANTHA, 48, MINNEAPOLIS

Comment:
When we acknowledge a painful event that happened within the family of origin to one sibling but not to us, it helps tremendously in healing wounds and strengthening the bond of friendship between us and our sibling.

Leave My Sister Alone

The movie *Something to Talk About* has several friendship themes, one of which—sisters as good friends—got me thinking about my younger sister. In the film, the younger sister feels great loyalty toward her older sister. When she learns about her brother-in-law's infidelities, she kicks him in the groin upon seeing him again.

I was reminded of an incident with my own younger sister when we were around eight and six. We had gone to a park near our house to play. Some older boys started hassling me. I remember Jane didn't miss a beat. She furiously struck out with her little fists and tiny feet, attempting to hit and kick one of the bigger kids, yelling at them to leave me alone. I was surprised by her bravery, but most of all by her loyalty to me. Until then I hadn't realized that she cared about me so much and was willing to put her caring on the line despite her small size. Over the years, her feisty, righteous indignation has come to my aid more than once, and I am always impressed and moved. She, the younger sister, has taught me a lot about bravery and loyalty. I know she will always be there for me.

—MK

Comment:

It makes an unforgettable impression on the older sibling when her younger sister unhesitatingly comes to her defense.

Built-In Best Friend

For the first time in twenty-eight years, I finally have my own identity. While such a statement may sound odd to most people, I am an identical twin. More important, I am an identical twin who has never lived apart from her twin until a couple of years ago.

My twin sister and I have been best friends and soul mates since the day we were born. We developed and spoke our own twin language until we were five. We began playing tennis at the age of six and played competitively through college, although we never wanted to compete against each other. We would reach the finals of many tournaments and then flip a coin to determine the victor. We would then play a few games and report a close score to the tournament desk, much to the dismay of the crowd, who wanted to watch "the twins" fight it out in the final.

My sister and I have often found it difficult fitting into a society that values individuality. Individuality is a quality non-twins take for granted. If all else fails in life, people consider themselves special because they are still different from everyone else in the world. The same does not hold true for us. We are both five feet six, weigh 115 pounds, and have blonde hair and brown eyes. We are still avid tennis players and love watching the grand slams on TV, most of the time connected by the telephone during exciting matches, but not saying a word.

We both love cooking, running, and working out. Our eating habits are the same, merely snacking during the day in order to save room for a late dinner. It has been said that we speak "in stereo," saying the exact same things at the same time. We are both extremely sensitive and caring and still shed tears at the sight of a homeless person or an underprivileged child. We love all the same authors, sports figures, musicians, and designers. We are both married, having gotten married one month apart in the same year, and like the old-fashioned role of taking care of our husbands. Up to this point in our lives, there has been nothing unique or individual about my twin and me.

We lived together our first twenty-six years and were roommates all four years in college. The reason we always gave for rooming together was that it would be just too difficult to divide our clothes. But, in reality, we never wanted to room with anyone else. While being a twin at times has its drawbacks (i.e., always being compared and referred to as simply "the twins," never by name), how could anyone else ever measure up to a person who wanted to do all the same things at the same time as you? We had each other as a built-in best friend. We had many friends in college and all the same friends, but none of them ever became "our" best friend.

After college, at the suggestion of somewhat concerned parents, we attempted to gain our own identities and moved to different cities. My twin moved to Los Angeles, and I headed cross-country to Washington, D.C. For the first two months, we visited each other every other weekend, until we realized that we had no interest in living apart. We were in our early twenties and felt this fun, new, exciting part of our life should be spent together. We'd be darned if anyone was going to try and keep us apart. So I promptly quit my job and moved to Los Angeles to be my twin's roommate once again.

Three years later, I met my future husband, who had just finished business school and was ready to move to San Francisco. My twin was also dating her future husband, who was from Los Angeles and intended to stay there. Once again, we found ourselves faced with the issue of living apart. This time, though, we both knew and were actually excited that we were finally ready to get out on our own and be our own person.

My first two years in San Francisco were not easy without my twin, but I am creating my own identity here. We speak on the phone at least six times a day, most of the time just to say hello and make sure the other is all right. But I am realizing that I am comfortable being separate for now. Our husbands have since assumed the role of a best friend for both of us, but my twin and I know that no one can, or ever will, replace the strong and unique bond of a sister, twin, and built-in best friend.

—LORI, 30, SAN FRANCISCO

P.S. Since I was interviewed over two years ago, much has happened in our lives. Once again, we realized we couldn't live far apart, and so Lisa moved up to San Francisco. Now we are both pregnant and due to deliver within three weeks of each other. Even though I'm having a girl, and my sister is having a boy, we have every hope that they'll be best friends as well.

Comment:
Some twins are natural built-in best friends, and their friendship supersedes all obstacles.

Express Your True Self

I have an identical twin sister, and she has become my best friend. Growing up, however, this wasn't necessarily the case.

As for most identical twins, our point of view, our sense of ourselves and our place in the world, were very similar. It was hard to cultivate a sense of who we were individually. We automatically grew up being compared.

To counteract this, our parents encouraged us to carve out different spaces for ourselves. Wendy was the artist and scholar, and I became the athlete. This way we could share the limelight but in diverse ways. As we got older, our lives went in different ways. Because we did not want to trespass on each other's turf, we made choices in reaction to each other. I became a landscape architect, and minister to plants; Wendy became an Episcopal priest, and ministers to people.

I remember that it wasn't until I was in graduate school taking my first drawing class and almost not being able to hold the pen (Wendy was "the artist," not me) that we really looked at our relationship. We realized that we spoke of each other as "best friends" but that we really weren't. We came to understand that in order to have a real relationship with each other, we needed to express and share our true selves instead of dancing around who we really were. We finally allowed ourselves to be vulnerable and real with each other, which led to the deep friendship we have today.

We worked hard on our friendship, and now we no longer threaten each other. We do not take our relationship for granted anymore, which is very important to remember for any friendship. Now we are "friends down to the bottom of our souls." Now we can walk in each other's paths in an inclusive way.

It's interesting how our lives are crisscrossing. I gave up my career to become a wife and a mother, and Wendy worked in the church. Recently she married and had a child, and so all the issues I've struggled with—giving up my job identity to become a homemaker, the challenges of parenting—she is now dealing with. She is learning from me just as I have learned from her religious life. Recently, I became a trustee of my church, something I would have been reluctant to accept if we hadn't confronted each other and healed our friendship.

Because of my deep relationship with my twin sister, I have high expectations of my most intimate friends. They must be willing to be vulnerable and true to their inner core with me, which naturally follows after a strong mutual trust has been formed. My journey of friendship with Wendy has helped me become a better friend.

—ABBY, 34, CLEVELAND, OH

Comment:
Other twins question their friendship and have to work harder to become deep friends.

Coming to Terms

I have finally accepted that my sister-in-law and I will never be friends. For many years, I have reached out to Joan. In countless ways I have tried to show Joan that I care about her, yet she has never responded in other than a perfunctory manner. For instance, when I leave phone messages, she rarely returns the call. I always remember her birthday with a nice gift and never receive a thank you. But since I love my brother and value close family relationships, I really wanted to be Joan's friend as well.

My brother loves music. For his birthday I gave him two tickets to his favorite musical, in which I had a small part in the chorus. We made plans to see each other at intermission. When we met, neither of them commented on the show. I finally asked them what they thought, and before my brother could open his mouth, Joan said it was "fine." Never another word. She didn't comment on the quality of the music, the costumes, the staging, my performance, or even thank me for the tickets.

My brother had invited me for a drink with them afterward, but when I met them, he said they had to get home. I expected they might say something then—a thank you or anything nice about the evening—but they just said good-bye. I walked off in a daze, feeling lousy and confused.

One of my close friends called me two days later to say that she'd seen my brother at a party. He'd told her about how great the show was and how excited he'd been that I had a part in it. Right then I had a long overdue wake-up call. In the past, I always came away feeling bad after spending time with Joan. I would wonder what I'd done wrong or what I could have done differently. I realized then that, no matter what, Joan will never be my friend.

I learned an important lesson from my unreciprocated "friendship" with my sister-in-law. Even with family, if the relationship drains too much energy because it is so one-sided, it's best to let it go. So I am pleasant to her, but I have stopped having any expectations of Joan.

—MARISA, 33, LOS ANGELES

Comment:

Because of what we were used to growing up, it may be natural to want to have good relationships with extended family such as a sibling's spouse. However, members of our extended family may have had different experiences within their own families of origin, and we have to balance our expectations with theirs. Understanding this may mean letting go of any expectations of there being a close friendship. It's O.K. to let go of expectations with regard to relationships that aren't working. Some friendships within the family are simply not realistic because of different upbringings, not to mention different natures.

Out on a Limb

I feel very lucky that my sister-in-law is one of my best friends. I guess because I have always been close to my sisters, I expected to feel that way toward my husband's sister. However,

I didn't think our relationship would be challenged the way it has been.

After five years as a single parent, my sister-in-law remarried. Everyone was very happy for her. However, the marriage quickly foundered. Jean's new husband had a terrible temper and made frequent physical threats. He was insanely jealous of her friends and even hated it when she worked in her garden. Jean shared this terrible reality with me within months of the wedding, and from that day on, we were in frequent touch. She so needed support, and I never gave a second thought to whether or not I could support her. In fact, I felt frustrated because I lived so far from her, but we talked a lot, and I wrote her letters reminding her how much I cared about her and how concerned I was about her safety and well-being. I told her if she needed me or her brother (my husband) to be there, we would be.

As I look back on my friendships, I don't believe I have ever told my friends enough about how much they mean to me, but I didn't hold back with Jean. I wanted her to know she could count on me, no matter what, because I felt she needed that kind of bedrock support to give her the strength to overcome her fear of leaving him. I also told her that while I didn't judge her because of what was happening, I didn't feel the marriage could go on.

I went further out on a limb. She had been reluctant to tell her parents, my in-laws, about her situation. While visiting them, I got the strong feeling that my mother-in-law suspected something was up. I decided to fill her in, and then I let Jean know what I had told her mother. I was concerned that she would feel I had betrayed her trust, but I felt strongly that the time for secrets was over, and I believe my instincts were right.

The older I get, the more convinced I am about the power of truth. This man, who pulled the wool over people's eyes with his pleasant public persona, counted on Jean's shame to keep her silent about his treatment of her. But the more people knew the truth and came to Jean's side, the stronger my sister-in-law became and the sooner she was finally able to put an end to this dreadful relationship.

She has since acknowledged how important my steady support was to her as she built up the courage to end the marriage. My husband—her brother—and I recently separated, and her support of me was unwavering. In fact, our friendship grew more during that period. When my husband and I reconciled, Jean and I celebrated as well because we knew our friendship would remain in the family. I am convinced the trust we forged during those difficult times solidified our friendship.

—Barbara, 44, Phoenix, AZ

Comment:

It is the positive experiences of friendship in our families of origin that motivate us to create friends within our extended families as well.

My Younger Sister's Best Friend

In my mind's eye, Cathy is still eight years old, with skinny legs like my sister's, a high-pitched voice, and the bluest eyes in the state of Maryland. In reality, she is now a grown woman in her late forties, with an important executive job and two step-grandchildren she dotes on. And though she hides them behind glasses, she has the bluest eyes in the state of Georgia.

I hadn't seen her for over twenty-five years until my sister and I had lunch with her in Atlanta a couple of years ago. Having lunch with my sister's oldest best friend was a trip down memory lane. The two of them share memories and experiences that go back almost as far as any of us can remember. Cathy, an only child, remembered things about me I didn't because, she admitted, my older sister and I were there to be looked up to and emulated. What we did made a bigger impression on her than it did on us.

I looked across the table at that lovely woman's face and could still see the cute little girl. I listened to her voice with its soft southern accent reflecting the many years she has spent in Georgia, and I can still hear her little-girl voice. Yet we now speak as grown women and laugh about very grown-up things. I was touched to see the evident affection between the two women—my sister and Cathy—affection that reaches farther back in time and is certainly more consistent than my own affection has been for my sister. In their company, I felt glad that she has had someone in her life like Cathy, who was there for her when I so often wasn't.

They told me about the time they had a big fight and stopped speaking to each other. Our mothers insisted the two girls get together to settle their differences. They did. Even our mothers thought their friendship was too important to let it unravel over some small disagreement. I also watched them laugh over the fact that, despite their saying they knew everything about each other, Jane had never told Cathy when she lost her virginity.

In some ways watching the two of them was like watching two fond sisters. They knew each other's jokes, facial expressions, what pushes each other's buttons. I came away from our time together envying Jane her long-standing friendship with Cathy, who was a far better friend to her than I ever was growing up. I do not have that kind of continuity with a nonfamily member. I came away with my own story expanded, enriched by Cathy's memories, realizing that far more people hold keys to our pasts than we might think. Most unexpectedly, I came away feeling a great appreciation of and fondness for both the child Cathy was and the woman she has become. No longer frozen in time, she is, as Jane's oldest best friend, a valued bearer of keys to both my sister's and my lives. I now feel she could be my friend as well.

—MK

Siblings' friends often have an extremely valuable perspective on our families of origin that can provide important insights. Sometimes childhood friends provide friendship siblings don't. Childhood friends, whether our own or our siblings', enrich our childhood memories and highlight how loving friendships that last into adulthood can help us understand who we were and where we have come.

My Older Sister's Best Friend

Valerie and my older sister, Sally, have been best friends for more than twenty-five years. They met in New York, where I also lived. They had many similar interests, not the least of which was that they were both writers. I saw Valerie many times, but as I look back over those meetings, I realize how reserved I always was with her. I never made an effort to get to know her because she "belonged" to Sally.

Valerie moved to the Bay Area in 1991. My husband, son, and I spent that summer in San Francisco. My sister, having made plans to visit Valerie before we knew we were going to be in town, ended up spending more time with me than with Valerie, who lived outside the city. Valerie was upset that she didn't see Sally as much as she had expected to. In Valerie's eyes Sally may have "belonged" to me.

Then we moved to San Francisco. Though Valerie still lived outside the city, she came to town, so I started seeing her from time to time. She had an extraordinary birthday party where she asked women friends to share the day with her. I felt immensely flattered that she included me. Yet I felt I was there more as a stand-in for Sally than as a friend of Valerie's. In my mind, she still "belonged" to Sally.

Valerie moved into the city, and we saw each other more frequently. She started a nonprofit organization helping women writers and asked me to be treasurer of the board. Several years earlier I had begun writing fiction, but I rarely let anyone read my stories. Valerie, the author of several books, is also an accomplished editor. I overcame my insecurities and asked if she would edit one of my stories. She did so, gave me great suggestions, and has since encouraged me in every way to keep writing fiction. The rapport between us grew, and Sally's spirit joined us every time.

Soon I moved less than a block away from Valerie. Responding to the panic in my voice on the phone when I said I couldn't figure out how to arrange the tiny living room, she rushed over. Within moments we had moved a chair here, the sofa there, put end tables in their proper places, and decided where paintings should go. We had a ball and agreed on everything. We laughed with great affection about the fact that Sally would be the last person either one of us would call to help us arrange furniture. In fact, that had always been my job in New York whenever Sally moved. Sally is not overly concerned with her space. Valerie and I agreed we need to have boxes unpacked immediately so that we can properly nest.

We fed each other's cats when one of us was away and took in the mail. We moved each other's car. We have borrowed books, cars, clothing, and even furniture from each other. Things a friend does for a friend. She has my house key and I have hers. We have long talks on the phone; we have lunch; we take walks. Things a friend does with a friend.

More than once I have called Valerie to find she is on her other line talking to Sally. I hop right off. Synchronicity aside, I honor their friendship. But more and more, irrespective of their relationship, I honor ours as well. After all, she comes with one of the best recommendations I could ever want. We love someone very special in common. I may still introduce Valerie as my sister's best friend, but now she's my friend as well. Happily, she "belongs" to both of us.

—MK

Comment:
When sisters are friends, their friends can easily become friends as well. As we age, the distinction between friend and sister can blur. If sisters have friends in common, it is like adding family. Mutual friends also help soften family patterns like those implied in birth order or other family roles siblings played out.

My Ex-Mother-in-Law's Grace

For many years after my first husband and I were divorced, my ex-mother-in-law and I remained friends. When I think of the really important friendships in my life, the ones that sustained me and carried me through some pretty difficult times, I always come back to this one. Beeza was my anchor; she treated me kindly and well even after I had remarried and was starting a second family with a new man who was no longer her son.

I remember she invited me, huge in my eighth month of pregnancy, out for lunch before our son was born. She sent me flowers in the hospital afterward and visited, laden with presents for the new baby. She was just as welcoming to our second son, born four years later. For a long time she kept in touch, giving us presents for birthdays and Christmas, and calling to check in and make sure all was well; I cherished her friendship.

Now the mother of three sons, I remember how my ex-mother-in-law treated me so kindly. Even though I'm sure I wasn't making my ex-husband, her son, very happy, I was the one who ultimately broke up the marriage, leaving my husband, an only child, and his parents to pick up the pieces of their lives. Now that I'm older and my son is grown with a wife of his own, I understand how hard it must have been for Beeza to keep her heart open toward me and to celebrate my new family with me, in spite of what had happened.

My ex-husband remarried and had three more children. Somewhere down the line, Beeza wrote saying she felt we should stop exchanging gifts. I knew she was saying good-bye, and I was sad. But I understood that with her loyalty to her son and his new family, there was no longer room for our friendship.

I will always be grateful to her for being my friend under very trying circumstances. I thank her for teaching me how to treat family—no matter what—with love and kindness. Should I be faced with a similar challenge, I will keep her example in mind and heart and hope I can act with as much dignity and grace as she did.

—LB

Comment:

Sometimes someone is able to look beyond her own pain and reach out, with love, to remain a friend, and give us the support we need despite difficult circumstances.

TWO

~

Shared Experiences and Values—Where Friendship Lives

We meet people in different situations, and frequently these circumstances create a foundation for a friendship to grow. Shared environments, interests, activities, and life experiences all contribute to the formation of friendship. Obvious settings are work, school, our children's schools, places of worship, and our neighborhoods.

Susie grew up in a small midwestern town, population four hundred, where it was like one big extended family. She remembers summer evenings going to the drive-in with twenty-three squeezed into one convertible. Her best women friends are still from her childhood. They all live in different places now, but once a year, without fail, they meet to ski and catch up with each other's lives. Susie feels their closeness has lasted because they grew up in such an inclusive environment where they shared similar values.

~

College roommates and best friends since the early sixties, Diedre and Linda have a real foundation of experiences together. Their friendship has survived geographical moves across the country, five marriages between them, children, and job changes. The friendship's longevity has given them a chance to look back over the years, laugh at who they were, and enjoy who they are today. Now, both in secondary education, this commonality of interest and profession adds an even greater dimension to the relationship.

Friendships also thrive because of common interests and activities. A love of art, travel, movies, or sports brings people with similar interests together, creating a common ground for friendship. Charitable activities like volunteering in a hospital, soup kitchen, or school can also foster friendship. Or we may meet friends through political causes or neighborhood issues.

Lynn's husband was transferred to Boston, and she arrived knowing no one. Her old minister had told her about a church where he had been a guest speaker several times. She started going and joined a Bible study group. There she met some wonderful new friends who got her volunteering in a homeless shelter, a particular interest of hers.

~

Peggy and Jane belong to the same book group and share a love of literature. When Edna O'Brien came to town, Peggy invited Jane to hear her read excerpts from her new novel. This enjoyable experience enlarged their friendship, and they signed up for the entire authors' lecture series.

In addition, friendship grows out of similar life experiences. Tragedy and difficult times such as financial problems, addictions, divorce, injury, illness, or death of a loved one provide common meeting grounds for friendship to grow. There is a natural flow of compassion and a greater understanding in these friendships because the friends involved have experienced first-hand what it feels like. They have felt each other's pain.

Sara and Pat both lost their mothers as teenagers. They feel they have a special bond they don't have with other friends who haven't experienced what they have. In fact, they discovered many similarities, mostly having to do with emotional difficulties in relationships. While similar interests and experiences certainly encourage and foster friendship, close friends also share similar fundamental values.

Lila and Maureen are friends, but Lila's children are older than Maureen's. In many conversations about their children, they have discovered they share similar parenting philosophies, which has made them feel very close to each other. Maureen can see in Lila's grown children how these values have worked, and she loves having a friend she can call who understands her values and has been there.

Close friends don't always have to agree about everything, but they have to have a similar desire to engage consciously in life.

Upstairs/Downstairs

When I was pregnant with my first child, my husband and I moved to Buffalo, New York, where I knew no one except his family. We started looking for places to rent but weren't having much luck, as a couple expecting a baby was not a landlord's first choice for a tenant.

One afternoon, driving down a small street, I was immediately charmed and said to my husband, "This street is exactly where I want to live." At that moment I spotted a "for rent" sign on a rambling double. We knocked and an attractive pregnant woman about my age, named Lucy, answered. She and her husband owned both the upstairs and downstairs flats and were living in one. She welcomed us in, and we signed the lease for the downstairs flat that day. Pregnant together and excited about becoming new mothers at the same time, we became instant new upstairs/downstairs friends. We were both thrilled beyond belief to have a friend with whom to share motherhood.

Three weeks later I gave birth to my first child, a daughter named Keller, who was born with Down's syndrome. Lucy, who has a degree in special education, was incredibly loving and supportive. She helped me through those first confusing days when I was coming to terms with my unexpected situation. One month later, Lucy went into labor and gave birth to her first child, a son, Michael, who also was born with Down's syndrome. While we had become close friends before this, because we were now both mothers of babies with special needs, our friendship became an unbreakable bond.

We remodeled the backstairs, making the two flats almost into one. We shared a baby monitor so we could cover for one another. We shopped for groceries and cooked for each other. When Lucy had to return to teaching, I watched Michael. Early on we found out that when you have a child with a disability, you cannot survive if you take it too seriously. We learned to laugh together. Even now we support each other; we're there to share our dreams, fears, and feelings with each other. As a result of our shared experiences, we're family. Lucy's children are as important to me as my own are.

In time, we both bought single houses. Now, instead of being upstairs/downstairs, we are across the street from each other. We had our second children at the same time, and while they are friends, it is Keller and Michael, now fifteen, who continue to be best friends. And it is because of them that Lucy and I became advocates for the integration of special children into mainstream education. We initiated the pilot program for inclusion of children with special needs into the Buffalo school system. The educators told us we were five years too early for such programming, but we persisted, and after three months our children were in the classroom with typical kids.

We have both become articulate as parents of children with special needs and have given many talks together. We have spoken to medical students and education professionals, showing them the parents' perspective and making them understand how we, the parents of disabled children, feel. We also want people to realize that we all need each other, and that we each have something to offer. Just because a child is different, this doesn't mean that he or she is not valuable. We learn from our differences. Keller and Michael have made us so much more aware of other people and what is really meaningful in life.

Coming back to my friendship with Lucy, I know we have accomplished so much because we have each other. But underneath our shared experiences runs a stronger current, and that is our belief in God. Even though I'm Episcopalian and she is Catholic, that difference doesn't matter because we're both devout in our faith. We believe God brought us together and through our common pain has given us these extraordinary "gifts"—our children. Our friendship is beyond coincidence; it happened because God reached out and clasped our hands together when I knocked on her door so many years ago.

—CHARLOTTE, 43, BUFFALO, NY

Comment:
Sometimes the right friend arrives at just the right moment to share deeply in our life's experiences.

Tried and True

Three of my closest friends are two women and a man I started a business with about ten years ago. This experience would have tested the strongest of friendships. But ours grew stronger because we never lost sight of the fact that we were partners, equal partners, and at the heart was respect for each other's special skills and talents.

While we were equal partners financially, I held the title of president, initially, anyway. Eventually, in order to grow the business, we had to sell a majority interest to outsiders. The new management was difficult. Under stressful conditions, I continued as president for a while and then was abruptly fired.

At that point, they made another one of us president. The male partner, a lawyer, left to start his own practice. The marketing expert also left under pressure from the new management. Eventually my successor was also fired.

Despite these events, we really pulled together to present a united front to these capricious owners. An injustice to one was an injustice to all of us. There was no place for envy, and never any thought of cutting a special deal that would hurt the others. Though we were all disappointed to have lost control of our creation, we wanted to ensure the best possible outcome for us and for our company because we were proud of it.

While none of us remains with the business, which is still successful, we are better friends than ever. Going through the challenges of starting a business, agonizing over the necessity of selling a majority interest, painfully realizing our new partners didn't have our best interests at heart, all these things drew us together. We are all doing other things now, but it wouldn't surprise me, if any one of us said, "I've got a great idea for a new business," we'd all drop what we were doing to climb on board. These friends proved that friendship and business can mix well.

—CATHERINE, 52, NEW YORK CITY

Only the Finest Ingredients

I love my job. What does this have to do with friendship? I work with some of my best friends.

We run a specialty cake bakery. The hours can be long, and the pay isn't great, but all day (or night) we have a ball: talking, laughing, and, of course, baking. In many ways I think the six of us really lucked out. We honestly do all love to bake and never seem to get tired of making beautiful desserts. However, the real secret ingredient is how well we all get along. It seems to be the perfect mix of personalities and temperaments.

If one of us is down about something, we take her on as a team project to cheer her up or help her think through her problem. If one of us doesn't feel like talking, we make a small joke out of it and leave her alone. We've had customers stop by and wonder how we get any work done, we do so much talking. I sometimes wish I were making more money, but I wouldn't trade a larger paycheck for my work buddies for anything, especially when I hear women complain about the people they work with, how competitive everyone is or the back-stabbing that goes on.

Talk about all the right ingredients! Not only do we make the most delicious cakes, but we have a great time doing it.

—DONNA, 31, ATLANTA

Comment:

Lucky is the woman whose workplace is enlivened by the joy of working with good friends.

Stitch and Bitch

When I was a young mother, I made friends with other mothers with children around the same age. There were about ten of us, and we'd meet once a week. Instead of being mothers alone, we were able to talk and learn about parenting, and our kids could play together. I remember feeling such a bond of love with these women. We were never competitive, never divisive; everybody was genuinely interested in what the others were doing. We supported each other; we laughed and cried together.

We were young and poor and enjoyed simple activities. One friend's mother had a pool, and so we'd all meet there. I remember sitting there in the sun sorting out hand-me-downs to pass out to our children. We learned to knit there. I think one reason we got along so well was that we shared a strong spiritual bond; we had good similar values and parenting styles.

As our children grew older and went off to school, we stopped seeing each other. But after a few years, we decided to meet again on a regular basis. We had an unspoken rule: If you had a problem, the Stitch and Bitch group would be there to help out. We organized a phone tree for emergencies, and whenever anyone had a problem, we'd all be there to help out. We've been through so much together. Two friends have had deaths of children, two husbands have died, there have been three divorces, two women with cancer, and many extended family members' deaths.

We've had our share of good times, too. We celebrate birthdays together. Three of us have birthdays close together in May. When the May girls turned fifty, we rented a Winnebago and went antiquing. The August girls had a wonderful celebration, too. Our husbands are friends, and over the years there were countless parties including all generations. We've attended christenings, graduations, weddings, and funerals together.

When I walk into a room where I know I'll see my friends from Stitch and Bitch, I'm excited. We're at different places in our lives now. Some of us have careers, others are involved in their community, but we're all committed to our families and our friends. Our children range from twenty-one to thirty-one, and we follow where they are going, too. We are all genuinely interested in each other in a kind and inclusive way. I don't know how I could have gotten through some difficult times if I hadn't had all these wonderful friends who have spanned my entire adult life. And I know for certain that they've made the good times all that more special and joyful.

—MIMI, 52, SAN FRANCISCO

The Moms' Connection

In my younger son's sophomore year, one of his friends hosted
a drinking party at her house when her parents were away. The
next morning, word of the party made its way to some of the
parents of the kids attending the party, including to my husband and me. Interested in nipping in the bud any trend
toward more such prohibited behavior, I suggested a group of us
get together. Nine mothers ended up meeting.

That was the start of what came to be known as the Moms'
Connection. Now, over four years later, the group has grown to
eighteen, and even though the kids have graduated from high
school, the moms continue to see each other, including making
trips to Arizona for reunions with one "member" who moved.
Some of my closest friends are now from the group.

Many of our kids played on teams. Our son played foot-
ball and baseball. Initially more interested in supporting our
son's participation than in the sport, my husband and I
became avid fans with the help of other Moms' Connection
members. We came to look forward to attending not just
home games but away games as well. We also started getting

together regularly to talk about parenting issues. There are so many aspects of raising teenagers that are challenging, such as dealing with driving, drinking, drugs, sex, academic problems, and so forth.

The chemistry is great within the group, a rapport that transcends the inevitable competitiveness among our children, disagreements they might be having with one another, and the like. In fact, my son and another member's son were very good friends for a couple of years, then had a huge fight. Despite their disagreement, the boy's mother and I remained friends. We were able to separate their issues from our own friendship. Moms in other classes have often commented on how lucky we were to have such good chemistry in the class.

Before we knew it, it was graduation day, and the games, parties, and tests were over for our children. For graduation, we gave each child a monogrammed laundry bag in the colors of the college he or she would be attending.

In September my son went east to college. On that first Saturday when his high school had its first home game, was I silently celebrating my freedom from the "obligation" of supporting the team? No. I was there with some of the Moms' Connection whose sons had also left for school, cheering on the team, giving and receiving comfort as it sank in to each of us that our "babies" had left home. Even in our children's absence, the Moms' Connection friendships go on.

—J, 54, PIEDMONT, CA

Comment:

Mothers need a support system of like-minded friends to help them with the important, sometimes overwhelming journey of parenthood.

Crossing the Line

For over six years, I saw a gifted, empathetic therapist who cried when I did and held my hand as I confronted the pain of my past. During this period of my life, she stood by my side as my deepest friend. At one point in my therapy, however, she crossed the line into a part of my personal life that made me very uncomfortable. When I brought it up in therapy, she tried to convince me she had not violated any boundaries.

We continued our relationship, but after a while I learned from a friend that she had repeated actions that we had talked about before that had made me so wary. This time when I asked her about it, she was not willing to be accountable in the way I needed her to be. I felt I had to end my work with her because trust had been broken. We parted precipitously. Because all of this happened so abruptly, at the end of a session that was never intended to be my last—and because we had worked together for so long—I guess I thought I would hear from her. But I never did. I had shared deep feelings and thoughts with her and felt our therapy work deserved a better ending.

Even when my father, the subject of many long discussions, died eight months later, she did not acknowledge my loss. I will always wonder why. I would love to have had the chance to honor all the work we had accomplished together. From this experience, however, I learned how important it is to say goodbye fully and well.

—LORRAINE, 38, PORTLAND, OR

Comment:

Boundaries are important between friends—no matter what kind of friendship it may be. Both sides need to be clear about them.

My Therapist, My Friend

Friendship is one of those gifts that just keeps on giving. Friendship is not a linear phenomenon but a spiral, a circle. In the tales of friendship that come first to my mind since I've been asked to write about friendship in my life, I see the connectedness of it: one story leads into another, which leads into yet another. For example, there is the story of Maria (names and other identifying features have been changed to protect her right to confidentiality), a woman who was my client when I was learning to be a marital and family therapist. I received an intake sheet with Maria's name on it and telephoned Maria to schedule a first appointment. A tearful but obviously intelligent voice responded to my call. Plaintively she wailed into the phone as I attempted to find out what she was wanting from therapy, "But can you help me?" I told Maria that I would try.

Two days later, Maria, a diminutive Puerto Rican woman, sat in front of me clutching a worn spiral notebook. She took the seat nearest the door as if ready to make a breakaway dash if things became too uncomfortable. I moved my chair nearer to hers to offer my energy and support. Her words were halting, filled with pain. She opened the notebook and read to me that her insides felt like one gigantic scream. Her life had been filled with what I would come to find out over the next year was unbearable pain. She'd been repeatedly abused sexually by her father, raped more than once, had faced discrimination in the workplace, was nearly penniless, barely functioning, and on the verge of homelessness. And now, on top of that, the one thing that was important to her in life was slipping though her fingers. Her teenage daughter, whom she had raised single-handedly after a short tryst with her wealthy employer had left her pregnant and estranged from her staunchly Catholic family, was leaving home. Maria was devastated that the girl's father, after years of having nothing to do with either of them, had recently returned to establish legal custody of her daughter. Maria, impoverished, had tried to represent herself in court but was no match for the attorneys her daughter's father had paid to get the job done. For Maria, this represented the final slap, the final shame that she was sure would finish her off for good.

I sat and listened to Maria. I listened with my ears, but more importantly with my heart. I too had, years before, been in Maria's position, having lost nearly everything I loved and held dear. I, too, had faced the loss of a teenage daughter through a divorce custody battle. Beyond clinical knowledge was the knowledge of pain and suffering of this caliber. I recalled how, during my pain, I had been fortunate to find a therapist with heart, who dressed beautifully and was beautiful and who sat with me when all I could do was cry. She was never too busy to return my scared calls. She offered me hope and life, just by being there.

As I listened and felt with Maria, tears came to my eyes. Many in my profession would say this was unprofessional, that I had let boundaries blur, let myself get too involved. My response allowed Maria to trust me in a way that she had never trusted another human being. With great courage she left her home each week to travel an hour by bus to keep our appointments. With difficulty, fear, and hesitancy she began to take some very small steps. She began to allow herself to scan the classified ads for some type of employment she felt she could do. She took a few college preparatory courses, walking miles through the Chicago night in order to save money on bus fare. Most important, Maria's ability to trust began to grow.

As summer approached, we both realized that I would be leaving the training program at the end of the year and that I would no longer be available to Maria. Maria was terrified of losing her connection with me. She told me that, although she knew I was her therapist, I was the only friend she had. For the first time in her life, in her relationship with me, she felt heard and understood. She had never experienced someone being available to her in her pain. She told me that she knew I was special that very first time she met me when I cried with her. That very first session she had a tiny glimmer of hope that maybe someone would understand and that from there she could move forward.

As termination neared, I remembered the poor good-byes I had said at various times in my life. I determined to give my clients and myself the opportunity to say good-bye with honor and integrity. As difficult as it was for Maria, she honored our work together by being willing to transfer to another therapist after I left the program. I heard reports from time to time that Maria was making progress—she had gotten a job, enrolled in college, her life was improving. Part of me wished that those tangible signs of progress had occurred when she was working with me. But when I truly reflect with my heart, I know that those changes could not have occurred without the work we had done together. It was time for both of us to move on.

The last day Maria and I met, I told her about my former therapist and how important that relationship had been to me. Maria replied that I had become that therapist. From time to time I would call my former therapist to report on my growth. The last time I called her, I learned that she had committed sui-cide. I grieved for the loss of this beautiful person who had given me such an exquisite gift. But then, I think, perhaps her work was done and it was time for her to move on. Strangely, when I think of her, I know that she still lives. She lives in me. Friendship is like that. Its gifts continue to grow long beyond the actual moment of the giving. The gift of receiving friendship is most fully realized when it is passed on.

—AMY, 48, RACINE, WI

Comment:

Sometimes the common ground that formed the bond for the friendship is no longer there. If that is the case, we have to complete the friendship well, acknowledging the place our friend held in our hearts and saying good-bye with kindness and dignity.

Deep Roots

One rainy afternoon my office phone rang and an unfamiliar voice introduced herself to me. It was a name I hadn't heard in about thirty years. Catherine had, in fact, been a summer friend long ago when my family had visited my mother's hometown in central New York. Her mother and my mother had known each other since their childhood, but Catherine's and my friendship hadn't gone beyond those brief summer visits.

She called to tell me that her mother had told her I was producing a Broadway musical and that she had seen it. She had absolutely loved the show and felt compelled to call me.

She said that if I had produced such a wonderful show, she knew she would still like me.

The show was about to close, and I was very upset about it. It meant a lot that we were reunited at such a tough time for me. We soon discovered we had more than just similar tastes in the theater. However, just as we were getting to know each other again, my family and I moved from New York.

Nonetheless I see her on just about every trip I make to New York, and the bond between us seems far stronger than the number of times we have gotten together would indicate. I think this partly has to do with the long shared history of our families, about which we have conversed at length. After all, our mothers knew each other, and their parents, and maybe even their parents. Even with our attention primarily in the present we enjoy sharing those deep roots. Besides, her love of my show forever endeared her to me as well.

—MK

> *Comment:*
> *It is wonderful when we reconnect with an old friend and realize that the bond between us transcends the common ground of childhood to celebrate and validate who we are as adults.*

Out of Sight but Not Out of Mind

Bettina was a college friend of my older sister's whom I knew casually. When she told my sister she was pregnant, Sally mentioned that I was as well. A few days later, Bettina called and told me she had learned about a terrific Lamaze teacher and suggested we sign up to be in the same class. Our sons were born about two weeks apart; mine was early, hers late. The boys are now teenagers, and over those years Bettina and I have become better friends despite our living far apart.

We have taken vacations with our families together and have rendezvoused for Thanksgivings at my sister's house. For a couple of years, we had weekend houses near each other in the Berkshires. She and her family have visited us since we moved from New York, where she still lives. On my annual spring trip to New York to see Broadway shows, I have eaten dinner with her and her family before taking her to a show.

Even if we talk infrequently, we always seem to pick up where we left off last time. We simply acknowledge our busy lives and move on to more important things. Neither one of us sees any point in feeling guilty.

I celebrate the genuine affection and respect between us and our rich shared history, starting with her friendship with my sister in college, cemented by the intense experience of childbirth classes, and strengthened by over a dozen years of having fun together. Our strong bond serves us well even if we're out of touch for a while. In general, I'd say we risk losing a friend if we don't maintain the relationship, but there are those special friendships that go on no matter what. These friendships aren't even dormant, because we know that out of sight doesn't mean out of mind between us. Bettina is one of those friends for me.

—MK

Comment:

When we move around, some friendships inevitably end. It takes effort for friends who are geographically far apart to maintain their closeness. The friendships we choose to continue are the ones rich with shared experiences and shared values.

THREE

~

Loving Kindness
in Friendships

*A*cts of kindness often mark the beginnings of a deep friendship, for nothing goes farther in building a strong foundation between friends than a thoughtful gesture. Close friends interact with love; they act kindly toward each other with no expectations of material benefit or reward. We can be truthful and trustworthy, but if our hearts are cold, then the very essence of the friendship is compromised.

If we were to remember how our good friendships started, it would probably not surprise us that most began with a kind thought, word, or deed. Stories abound of loving and kind things friends do for one another.

Jane's older brother was diagnosed with a brain tumor. He still lived in their hometown a thousand miles away, and she couldn't get away, so her friends stepped in and organized a therapy swim group they called The Flippers. Three days a week they picked him up and went swimming with him, each friend taking turns swimming by his side. Jane, with her friends' loving support, felt involved in his recovery even while far away.

~

Kathy arrived at Rebecca's front door unexpectedly, her arms overflowing with fresh-cut roses from her garden. Kathy was leaving town for a while at the height of rose season and she wanted her friend, who loved roses but had no garden, to enjoy them.

Val knew Mary was having twelve people for dinner as a fund-raiser for her son's school. Unsolicited and knowing of her friend's resistance to asking for help, she offered to assist in the kitchen. She ended up staying the entire evening till the last dish was washed and dried.

Friends help out in times of need; they drive a carpool, run an errand, help a friend move, or lend a sympathetic ear. The magnitude of what we do for our friends doesn't matter. What does is acting from a place of love that encourages closeness and kindness. The more we truly love, the more being kind is simply the way we are.

It is also important that we are thoughtful and aware of what is going on in our friends' lives.

Sandra had coffee with her close friend Lena, who casually mentioned that her tenth year of sobriety was coming up soon, but then Lena quickly changed the subject. Later, Sandra called her and told her how impressed she was with what Lena had accomplished since becoming sober. Lena thanked her friend for her supportive phone call.

We also need to be clear about our friends' needs. Certain friends may not welcome advice when they have a problem; instead they want their friends simply to be present and listen. Others like being advised and feel supported by that input.

Whatever the parameters of the friendship are, friends make a difference by understanding and empathizing. hey enlarge our horizons and open doors that might otherwise remain shut. They inspire, encourage, and celebrate our triumphs. They also help us claim new parts of ourselves.

When Peggy was carpooling to work with her friend, the song "She's So Fine" by the Chiffons came on the radio. Peggy started singing along. Sally, who had sung in her church choir for years, told her what a nice voice she had. Peggy was stunned, but Sally's compliment led Peggy to find a voice teacher, a secret fantasy she'd had for years. Sally's encouragement opened up a whole new area of creative expression for Peggy.

~

After a long conversation, Alice turned to Melinda and said, "With your empathy and insight into people and your listening skills, you really should become a therapist." Melinda, who had never acknowledged this talent in herself, went on to become a successful child psychologist.

Friends also help us reinforce values.

When Juliana saw Joan take a stand for a friend, it reminded Juliana how important that value was for her.

Mary watched a friend patiently cook dinner with her child "helping," and it inspired Mary to do more of the same with her children when she saw how well the child responded.

~

Martha always loved her friend Gretchen's clothes and felt she had little style in comparison. One day she told Gretchen how she felt, and Gretchen immediately offered to take her shopping and help her develop her own sense of style. Both women felt great afterward. Martha was thrilled that she had a friend who wanted her to look her best.

Friends add fun and laughter to our lives and fill up those empty spaces in our hearts. In a world overflowing with serious problems and disasters, it's wonderful having friends who comfort us and lighten our journey.

After a ski accident, Kris had to move back home to recover. At twenty-two, she was paralyzed emotionally and physically. She spent all day calling her friends for sympathy. But it was Rosie, unemployed and struggling to make ends meet, who flew to Los Angeles from Miami and got her laughing again. Being with Rosie reminded Kris of who she really was before the accident and who she wanted to be again.

The picture is not complete without mentioning meanness, which is also ever present in our lives. It is when we are afraid that we are most susceptible to our mean side. Most unkind actions stem from an uneasy and fearful place in ourselves, a part of us that we haven't spent enough time nurturing and caring for. Whenever we feel competitive with a friend—over appearance, financial success, possessions, accomplishments, even romance— we create a damaging win/lose dynamic. How important it is to understand that a friend's win is our win as well.

There are varying degrees of meanness—someone can sit still and not help a friend who is suffering in some way; or remain silent when speaking up for a friend would make a difference; or consciously act in a mean-spirited, competitive way by undermining, scapegoating, or backbiting.

Wendy and Ann were friends, as were their young sons. When the two women had a falling-out that had nothing to do with the children, Ann stopped inviting Wendy's son over and would no longer allow her son to play at Wendy's. She also made a concerted effort to pull other friends away from Wendy's son. He was devastated. Wendy, seeing him so upset, vowed never to use anyone, especially a child, as a pawn in any problem "friends" might have.

~

Helen and Maude were in a writing group together. Helen got an article published in the local paper. Maude was jealous of her friend's success and made comments to mutual friends belittling the accomplishment and saying it was probably because she had connections at the paper. Helen heard about what Maude had said and was sad that her friend felt threatened.

When Carolyn was feeling upset about her job, she called Josephine for support. Josephine listened for a few minutes and then said she had another call. The next time Carolyn called her, Josephine interrupted and said, "When you're feeling better, call me and we'll go out and have a beer." This final comment made Carolyn realize she no longer wanted a mean friend like Josephine in her life.

Recognizing when we are unkind and taking responsibility for our actions by apologizing, we go a long way toward repairing any damage and toward making ourselves more aware so that the next time we will behave lovingly and kindly. Being mean hurts us as much as it hurts the person to whom we've been mean. Being kind lifts us up as much as it lifts up another. With love at its root, kindness always furthers friendship.

Just Be Kind

I grew up in Nashville, Tennessee, in a large, eccentric, cohesive family. My father's advice to us was to live our lives in such a way that we could look anyone in the eye and tell 'em to go to hell. He didn't care much about folks in general, but he did care about the family. My parents built a house on the block adjacent to my grandparents' rambling antebellum property. Three of my father's first cousins and one of his sisters built their houses on our same block. My brothers, sisters, cousins, and I moved through each other's houses as if they were our own, watched over by an elder generation of brothers, sisters, and cousins. I remember my father's cousin Elsie saying, "I didn't know Brother wasn't my brother until I was thirteen." We were close then and still are.

There was, however, one person who taught me to consider others outside the closed periphery of my immediate family and friends. Her name is Ruth. She, through example, has shown me that a person is not just a single entry on one's family tree. The human family is a vast collection of souls in various and sundry bodies, in a splendid array of colors and sizes. The South was a segregated place in the fifties of my childhood. Ruth's farm was not. It was a gathering place for a kaleidoscope of people. Everyone brought something to the table, something of value, a different perspective.

I now live in San Francisco, a wonder of diversity. New situations present themselves every day, some good, some bad. I think often of what Ruth taught me: Be kind, just try to be kind. I remember a simple incident that brings her words into sharp focus. Last Christmas, my son, daughter, and I headed into a record store. Outside the entrance stood a disheveled panhandler. As we walked past him, he said, "Thank you." As soon as we got inside, my ten-year-old son asked me why he had said that. I said it was because I had smiled at him.

When we left the store, all three of us beamed at the panhandler, and then we all wished each other Merry Christmas. No money changed hands, but I knew that our treating each other kindly made a big difference to all of us. I am a much nicer person because of what Ruth taught me. It is a lesson learned on my part, a conscientious effort. Being generous of spirit is not easy. I was blessed to have had Ruth show me how.

—EDITH, 44, SAN FRANCISCO

Comment:

No matter how different we may seem to each other on the surface, underneath we all yearn for the same thing—to be treated with kindness and compassion.

Almost My Mother

One of my mother's best friends died suddenly a few days ago. Her death breaks one more link in that chain that connects me to my mother. Marjory was ninety-one and had led a long and full life; she had loving children, grandchildren, great-grandchildren, and many friends. But she always had room in her life and in her heart for me. She was the mother I'd lost when I was twenty-two; I always knew she was there for me, a warm, embracing presence, solid and indestructible.

She made Bill and me feel as if we were part of her family. We were included in many of her parties. We had summer houses across the street from each other, and often we'd have drinks or dinner together. When our sons were growing up, Marjory acted as if they were her grandchildren, sending them presents, following their progress as they learned to walk and talk and then head off for school. She was thrilled with their successes and ready to pick them up when they fell. They learned how to swim in her pool; her house was always open to us.

She was elegant, energetic, always interested in her family and friends. Because of her unfailing enthusiasm about life, people of all ages surrounded her. She frequented the ballet, opera, symphony, art museums, gave wonderful dinner parties, and often went out to lunch. My friend Gretchen reminded me that once when we were having lunch together, we saw Marjory and Mrs. Goldie; Gretchen said that I went over to their table to greet them. I said how much I hoped I would look and act exactly as they did when I was their age. Marjory was what I'd call ageless.

When I had a problem, I'd talk to her about it. She was good at listening and even better at giving advice. She had a great sense of humor, and many times she got me laughing when minutes before I had been crying. She used to say to me in a kidding way, "Linda, I could never be your mother; you cry too much." But in the same breath, she told me that she herself couldn't cry, and she wished sometimes she could, so she was glad I did it for her.

Because Marjory was of the old school, we rarely talked directly about emotions. Recently, though, we were sitting together, watching my seventeen-year-old son, John, who was surfing. I turned to her and said, "Marjory, I hope you know that I love you very much." There was a silence and then she turned to me and said, "I know you do, dear, and I love you, too." Oh, how I shall miss her and her generous friendship.

—LB

Comment:
When we have a loving and open heart, age makes no difference between friends. Everyone has something to learn from—and to give to—everyone else regardless of age.

Sharing Unbearable Pain

The young son of a close friend of mine died unexpectedly from a cerebral hemorrhage. The death of a child is unbearable; it is beyond imagining how painful this is for the parents and the entire family.

A week after his death, I went on a long walk with my friend. As we were walking, I began praying and asking God to give me the right words to say. I knew how devastated she was feeling. Was there a way I could lift any of her sorrow?

She went through the tragedy, detail by detail, not sparing herself or me anything of what had happened. She doubted herself for not taking him to the doctor sooner; she blamed herself terribly for not being able to revive her son when he had his fatal seizure. Even though I told her she had done all anyone could have done and much more, I felt she couldn't hear my words through her grief and feeling totally responsible.

We walked on for a while in silence, and suddenly I said, "Be kind to yourself. Be kind to yourself." She turned to me and said, "You're my only friend besides my mother who has said that to me." I knew she'd continue her relentless self-scrutiny, but I hoped that later, maybe later, she'd remember these words and find some solace from them.

At the end of our walk she told me that even though the death of her son was incomprehensible to her, she believed in goodness coming back again into her life. She wondered if in three months' time, when everyone had gone back to the business of everyday living, she'd be able to pick up the phone and ask for help. I told her that someday she might be needed to help another person through the unbearable darkness. I went home to my husband and cried, saying I had never felt so helpless in a friendship before. Later when my friend called, I went over to her house and sat with her and felt perhaps I was making a difference.

—LOUISE, 44, SAN JOSE

A Loan Becomes a Gift of Friendship

I hadn't heard from an old friend in quite a while. I knew she had left her husband and moved across the country, but she had never let me know her new address, so I was not able to reach her. Out of the blue one day, she called. Things were not going well for her. She was unemployed and was almost destitute financially. She thought she might have to go to a women's shelter. I couldn't believe it. This was a bright, well-educated woman who had worked in challenging positions until she had children, and then she and her husband had decided it was best for her to stay home. Now, she couldn't find a job, and her husband, retaliating for her departure, wouldn't help her.

I offered to lend her some money. My husband and I are not rich, but I couldn't stand the thought of her having to go to a shelter because she didn't have any money. Reluctantly she accepted my offer, and I fired off a check to her. Several months went by and the check never cleared. Finally I heard from her again. She sounded so much better. She had found a job, and while it didn't pay well, she was back on her feet.

I asked why she had never cashed the check. She said that she had kept it in a drawer like an insurance policy and as a symbol of our friendship and my faith in her and my caring for her. She told me my gesture of friendship had given her that extra boost she needed to start the journey back up from the bottom, and that gift was far more important than any money I might have lent her.

—MK

Comment:
Even though money can be an issue that causes problems between friends, if it is given or lent from a loving place—and with a clear agenda—everyone wins.

I'm Here to Make Your Beds

Erna became one of my dearest friends on that day, in May 1953, when my husband, three small children, and I moved into our house in Syracuse, New York. In the chaos of unpacking alone, my husband away on a business trip and the three girls running in and out of the new house, I heard a knock at the door and a cheerful "Hello!" with a distinct Texas lilt to it. In waltzed Erna, a petite, attractive blonde about my age with the kindest blue eyes, saying "I'm your next-door neighbor, Erna Northup, and I'm here to make your beds." With that thoughtful gesture (five beds and no fitted sheets!) a lifelong friendship began that is still going strong over forty-five years later.

She was, in fact, the queen of the unexpected but much appreciated offer of help. When I had a dinner party—whether or not she was invited—she pushed over a wheelbarrow, stacked it with the dirty dishes and took them to her kitchen, where she had that marvelous new invention, the dishwasher. Later she returned with the clean china and silver.

One incident stands out in my memory. My aunt died and my husband and I had to go to her funeral, a good four-hour drive away. Just as we were leaving, one of my daughters suddenly became very ill. I called Erna immediately, and she stepped right in. I really didn't want to leave because I knew Mary was very sick, but I was able to go because I knew that Mary, who ended up being diagnosed with scarlet fever, couldn't have been in better hands.

I loved having a next-door neighbor like Erna. When my husband was transferred to Maryland five years later, Erna went with me to house hunt. How I wish she could have been buying the house next door! Despite the distance between us, however—and we both moved several times—we remained close friends, visiting whenever we could and writing letters. I have never forgotten how thoughtful she was to me during those busy years of raising a family with very little money.

Finally, upon retirement, we ended up living within an hour of each other. A few years ago, both widows, we took our first trip together. We ended up being the perfect roommates.

Erna, who had become quite deaf, turned her hearing aid off at night. It was a good thing, because my daughters never stop telling me how loudly I snore.

—CATHERINE, 81, SARASOTA, FL

Comment:

Sometimes a friend appears out of nowhere, delighting us with an unexpected act of kindness. We never forget friends who demonstrate such loving kindness.

The Gift of Listening

My friends, especially my women friends, are invaluable to me. What I have written here is just one example of what friendship means to me.

When I think of friendship, I can't help but think of Toni, because she had all of the attributes I look for in a friend—loyalty, trust, sense of humor, and a willingness to "be there" for me. I remember one specific incident when Toni gave me a wonderful "friendship present"—a present that was so simple, and yet it was notable, because in my experience it was unusual!

Her present was that of listening—listening to the details of a trip I'd just taken to a women's conference. People usually ask, "How was your trip?" You say, "Fine." And that's the end of it. But I remember how Toni sat and listened unhurriedly to every detail—of speakers I'd heard, places I'd visited, and people I'd met, asking pertinent questions along the way. When I finished, I knew I'd been given a rare gift! That was twenty years ago, and I've never forgotten it or Toni.

—GAYLE, 54, SACRAMENTO, CA

Comment:
When we sit still and silent by a friend's side and listen, we are giving her a simple but priceless gift.

Another Pair of Ears

I have been having a very hard time with menopause. Recently, I was scheduled to have a new procedure done, the purpose of which was to find out why I was having so many problems and complications. I was becoming more and more confused because it seemed that every doctor I talked with had a different idea or opinion about what I should do.

A very good friend of mine who had had breast cancer some years before called me up and quietly said that she was available to accompany me to the doctor's whenever I needed her to. She said that when she was having her medical problems, her best friend went with her to the doctor's because she was so upset she couldn't absorb what they were saying. Her friend was later able to help her interpret and understand what had been discussed during the meetings. My friend said simply that she was offering me "another pair of ears." I cannot begin to tell you what a difference that made for me.

—KATHY, 50, SANTA FE

A Toast Nobody Heard

I recently hosted a birthday luncheon for two good friends and seventeen other friends at a lovely restaurant in town. During the meal, I stood up and clinked my glass so that I could make a toast to our friends. I wanted to say some things about women and friendship. Everyone went right on talking. I clinked my glass again, thinking they hadn't heard me the first time. They finally quieted down enough for me to began the little talk I had prepared. I said that one of the good things about women friends is that you can have more than one, as opposed to being in a relationship with only one man. At that point several of my guests (many of whom have been single for years) started laughing and talking among themselves.

I wasn't finished with my toast, so I clinked my glass a couple more times to get their attention again, but finally I gave up and sat down, feeling terrible. Though I made light of it at the time, I couldn't help it when tears came to my eyes. No one cared enough to listen to what I wanted to say to honor our friends on their birthdays.

Later that afternoon, one of the guests of honor called and asked if I was O.K. She was the only one who had seen how upset I was, and while she hadn't felt strong enough to take control of the group and insist that they listen to me, at least she felt bad enough to want to find out how I felt about what had happened.

Sometime after the luncheon, I came across a wonderful essay Brenda Ueland wrote in the late fifties entitled "Tell Me More." Ms. Ueland said, "When we are listened to, it creates us, makes us unfold and expand. Ideas actually begin to grow within us and come to life. . . . It makes people happy and free when they are listened to. . . . Suddenly you begin to hear not only what people are saying, but what they are trying to say and you sense the whole truth about them."

Her observations validated my feeling hurt that my friends would not listen to me and made me reassess my friendships. I now want friends who see me, hear me, and understand how much it hurts to be dismissed.

—Patricia, 48, Chicago

Let Everyone's Light Shine

Is it too much to hope that our friends will celebrate our strengths and encourage us to go out in the world and shine? Why are some people so threatened by others' talents or achievements? Is it because they have trouble coming to grips with their own power that they cannot acknowledge it in their friends? I wish we could realize that another person's success does not in any way diminish us; rather we are all better for it.

I have a friend, Alex, whom I've known for over thirty-five years. Her parents were great friends of my parents, and so our friendship began even before I married her best (male) friend from high school. We've been through a lot together, and my husband and I have always stood by Alex, considering her to be one of our closest friends.

After my mother's death years ago, Joan, Alex's mother, opened up her arms to us, welcoming us in as unofficial members of her family. Since I'm an only child, to be included in such a close-knit family as this meant so much to me, and Joan became the mother I'd lost. When she died, I was devastated.

Since Alex was on a trip when her mother died, I sent a short piece I'd written about Joan to her granddaughter, who showed it to her father and her siblings. They all loved it and asked me if I would read it at the funeral.

I said I would be honored to and rushed down to the church to practice once before the service the next day. As I stood up at the podium and began to read, I noticed two women I'd never seen before seated in the front pew. The church was otherwise empty. I hesitated but then began. At the end they clapped, and when I walked by, they were both crying. I left feeling happy that what I had written about Joan had touched someone else.

When I got home, there was a message on my answering machine saying that the family no longer needed me to read at the service. I pieced together what happened and came to the conclusion that it was my friend, Alex, who upon her return had said no. I realized then that she felt threatened by what I had written and did not want to be upstaged in any way. She also was not able to allow me to shine in this small way. I felt an almost unbearable sadness, sadness that our friendship wasn't what I thought it was, sadness that she could be so insecure and small-spirited, and sadness that she denied me the chance to stand up and celebrate my friendship with her mother. Oh, how much it would have meant to me to speak out loud those words of love that I felt not only for Joan but for my mother as well.

Friendship is all about love and wanting the best for each other. I was dependent on Alex being kind-hearted because I never thought she would be otherwise. Is it too much to ask of ourselves to act in a loving way even when we do feel insecure? What a gift of friendship she would have given me had she allowed me to read at her mother's funeral. Not only would it have healed some of my wounds surrounding the death of her mother and my mother, it would have touched all of us there at the service. I am reminded of some words of Nelson Mandela, who wrote, "There is nothing enlightened about shrinking so that other people won't feel insecure around you. . . . As we let our own light shine, we unconsciously give other people permission to do the same."

What I learned from this experience is just how important it is that a friend's success belong to all of us. I keep with me wonderful memories of Joan. I'd like to believe that she heard me speak of love and friendship when I was practicing that morning in the church, with the sun streaming through the stained-glass windows in vibrant ribbons of color.

—LESLIE, 44, NEW ORLEANS

Comment:

One of the best ways we can be true to a friend is to celebrate her talents and her successes and to encourage her in any way we can. When we acknowledge a friend and give her a chance to express herself, we are lifted up. Too often our insecurity comes out, and we somehow see our friend's win as our loss. When we deny a friend her win, we do, in fact, become the loser. We close down and are diminished, and our own talents and skills stay stuck in that dark place. In reality, when our friend excels, we are uplifted as well and our kind and loving words and support bring as much joy to us as to our friend. God-given talents are meant to be developed in each of us and in turn to be shared with everyone. The true friend is there to encourage her friend to shine as brightly as she can.

Balcony People

A good friend and I play competitive tennis together. Recently we were invited to represent Northern California at the Intersectionals. Teams from across the United States come and compete against each other. It was an honor to be asked, but at the time, I wasn't feeling very well. The thought of flying to Tucson and playing in 90-degree weather was not very appealing to me.

My partner, Andi, said she'd like to go but that if I didn't, she'd understand. I couldn't decide. She never pressed me; instead she gave me space in which to make up my mind. But when the deadline for our saying yes approached, she did call and remind me that if I didn't want to go, another team, which just happened to be our biggest rival, was waiting and ready to replace us. I then agreed to go to the competition.

Not only did we have a wonderful time, we ended up winning for the Northern California fifties division. I told my friend how much I appreciated her handling of this situation. She had been straightforward about wanting to go but not in an over-bearing way. She had understood my ambivalence. She also knew that we would be passing up an exciting and memorable opportunity, should we not go on the trip. So she had decided to take a risk and force my hand.

In looking back on this, I am thrilled that Andi and I went to the Intersectionals and proud that we won. She showed me that sometimes it is important to take the lead in a friendship and help a friend get to a place she might not have gotten to on her own.

Andi is what my friend Kaki calls a "balcony person." What she means by that is a friend who is up there in the balcony encouraging her friend, cheering her on, and clapping loudly for any success she has.

Kaki sits in my balcony as well. When I returned from winning the Intersectionals, she called and invited me over for coffee. She said she wanted to hear all the details of the tournament. When I walked into her living room, I was surprised by many of my friends, whom she had gathered together to congratulate me and share my excitement over my victory. Once I got over my shock, I immediately wanted to hide and run away. I felt embarrassed and overwhelmed by so much attention.

Kaki took my hand and gently drew me into the smiling group. I was surrounded by all my friends, who were laughing and congratulating me. At that instant Kaki's and my friendship went to a deeper level and I understood the true meaning of what it means to be a "balcony person."

—LB

The Chosen One

One of my dearest friends died recently of cancer. I had known Eleanor since the early fifties, when we were both in our thirties and raising young children. Eleanor and her husband hand-picked my husband and me to be their friends. They explained that they had lots of acquaintances but not many friends and asked if we would like to cultivate a friendship. Two other couples were also asked, and for the next five years, I believe I was happier than I had ever been because of that group of friends. There was something about being chosen that got everything off to a great start.

We four couples were inseparable, and the husbands and wives seemed equally compatible. Eleanor, in particular, however, may have been my favorite person in the whole world. When she was dying, I cried over the phone to my daughter and told her I couldn't imagine living in the world without my friend. This was a very strong sentiment in spite of the fact that we may have seen each other only once a year for almost forty years.

In some ways Eleanor was the kind of person I wish I had been—fearless, determined, optimistic, and endlessly enthusiastic.

With her flashing, never-miss-a-thing blue eyes and pure white hair from the time she was thirty, Eleanor was someone who, when she made a wish, made sure it came true. Furthermore, Eleanor and her husband had the kind of partnership I wish I'd had, for they were a near perfect match in terms of passions, intellect, and wanderlust.

Despite the financial limitations of their chosen work—he was a private school teacher and she was a nurse—they managed their finances brilliantly so that they could travel extensively. They lived abroad many times, for months at a time. I admired them so much and envied them, too.

I still feel so lucky that Eleanor and her husband chose us way back when, though they always made it very clear that the affection was mutual. Eleanor always seemed to see the best in me. And as with everything else in her life, she went after it and mined it for all it was worth. I think Eleanor always brought out my best, and what greater gift can one friend give another? I still miss her very much, but I like to think of it as a short-term separation, for one day, we'll have all the time we want to be together.

—CATHERINE, 81, SARASOTA, FL

Comment:

How wonderful is the woman who brings out the best in her friend. When we see a friend's gold, we are encouraging our friend to live out her potential and to shine as brightly as she can.

Heaven Sent

A wonderful friend came into my life right when I most needed her. Carol was a friend of my sister's, but I never really knew her until I was married and moved with my husband to Kansas City. We had a beautiful new baby, my husband had a new job, and we were embarking on an exciting life together. I met Carol, and her friendship just added to the happiness I was feeling.

Soon after our move, however, my life changed drastically. I had a seizure—I fell, lost consciousness, and really hurt my head. After many tests, I was diagnosed with a rare form of epilepsy that didn't respond to the normal drugs. Over the next six years I had seizure after seizure. I never knew when they would happen, and so this health problem absolutely dominated my life. I couldn't drive, I couldn't be left alone with my child, and I didn't feel like going out very much for fear that an accident would happen.

Carol, who was a very new friend at the time and going through a painful divorce, simply stepped in and never stopped helping me. She drove me to doctor after doctor, she helped me sort out all the medical opinions, and she never stopped trying to find out any new information that might help me. One day she called to say she'd heard of a doctor on the West Coast who specialized in my problem. She insisted that we fly there immediately. Discovering that there was an experimental operation that at times had an 80 percent chance of success, she, along with my husband, encouraged me to go for it. She was nearby during the operation and at my side afterward.

Two years have passed, and I am seizure-free. Carol's consistent caring, her love, her being there by my side, her never making it seem as if it were a hardship for her to spend so much time with me—all these gifts I will carry with me forever. Without her as my friend, I know I would not have made it to where I am today.

This positive experience with Carol caused me to reflect on certain friendships I've had where friends have exhausted me with their incessant emotional demands. I am so aware now that friendship is a two-way street. I don't know how I can ever be as good a friend to Carol as she has been to me, but I'm sure going to try.

—JANIE, 33, KANSAS CITY, MO

Comment:
Sometimes an angel comes into our life—out of the blue—when we need her most. Receiving this loving care can inspire us to go out and be an angel to others.

Favors and Friendship
Go Hand in Hand

It wasn't until I became friends with Kate that I learned how important it is to be able to ask for help. Before knowing her, I'd found it difficult to ask a favor of a friend. But she set an example for me by asking if I could pick up her son sometimes or if he could stay at our house after school when she had a later appointment.

I was happy to do these things, but still reluctant to ask her for anything. I was holding back from showing her that I was anything less than a supermom. I realize now that I was just afraid of admitting I was human, afraid that if I showed her I couldn't do it all by myself, I would be revealing too much of myself. One day she said that she really wished I would ask her for help sometime. I realized then that the path toward close friendship involves connections and the lending of each other's support. None of us is an island alone.

I know some women who would never dream of asking a favor of someone else; they are the ones who like to be in control and invulnerable. I've come to understand that in opening ourselves up, we become stronger and more intimate with others. Because of my experience with Kate, I was able to pick up the phone and call a friend 3,000 miles away and ask her if she could drive my son to his first day of boarding school. She said, "Yes, I'd love to. My son has just left for college, and I'm feeling a little lonely. There is nothing that I'd rather do."

When I put down that phone, I felt terrific because I had taken a chance and asked a big favor of my friend. Instead of her regarding my request as an imposition (which it was) she enthusiastically agreed to help me and my son and viewed the opportunity as a gift to herself as well. Because Kate was so generous with me, it has made me less reluctant to ask for help when I need it and more enthusiastic about helping when asked.

—LB

Comment:
Allowing ourselves to be vulnerable and ask for help is an important building block in the bridge of friendship.

Balancing the Scale

Some friends never ask for help; others ask for favors a lot and rarely reciprocate. Special circumstances when such an imbalance exists are to be expected—when a friend is sick or there's been a death in the family. We all reach out to help at such times, doing so gladly and with no thought of reciprocation.

Things can get touchier, however, when favors become an everyday thing. As an only child, our son loves having friends over. My husband and I have been extremely flexible, encouraging him to invite friends over to play, spend the night, do things like go to the movies, or even take trips with us.

For several years, he had a buddy he played with a lot. Andy came over time and again, but our son was never invited to his house. The imbalance became noticeable. I mentioned it to my husband and even suggested to our son that he might want to start playing with other kids since he was never invited back by this boy.

Meanwhile, Andy's mother and I had become friendly, and one day we had lunch. She brought up how much her son enjoyed doing things with us and expressed her appreciation of the opportunities we had given him. Then she asked if something was wrong because she had noticed I had become more reserved recently. With that opening, I said that I was feeling a bit taken advantage of; that we had Andy over so much and that our son was never invited to their house. Deborah may have been surprised at what I said, but she took it very well. We talked about her family situation: two other kids in the family; a relatively small home; her husband having his office at home; and Deborah, in her late forties, in her residency. She was either never home or was exhausted when she was. The imbalance was more understandable.

Despite all those circumstances, over the ensuing months, she made a great effort to invite our son to do more things with Andy. She had us over for a delicious shrimp dinner. Her husband went out of his way numerous times to bring our son home from school. Plus, Deborah never stopped expressing their appreciation for what we were doing for Andy.

The family moved at the end of the school year, and I know our son misses his buddy. While the scales were uneven in terms of who had done what with whom and how many times, our talk made a big difference. It moved both of us: me from a place of growing resentment to one of understanding and Deborah to a greater awareness that imbalances have to be acknowledged, appreciated, and redressed when possible. Besides, as an added benefit, our honest talk made us better friends.

—MK

Comment:

Friendships thrive when help is a reciprocal part of the relationship. We all want to feel needed. Helping a friend and allowing a friend to help us satisfy those needs. Knowing we can count on a friend's help and vice versa strengthens the loving bond between us in a healthy way. In communicating clearly, the scales can be brought back into balance.

FOUR

~

Truth and Honesty
in Friendships

*T*ruth begins with ourselves. The greater our own honesty and authenticity, the more we will expect that in our friendships. The more integrated we are as to our own feelings and beliefs, the more that translates into speaking our truth to friends.

We want to feel we are making a difference in a friend's life. To do that we need to be real and vulnerable. Friendships based on mutual truth telling deepen as each friend tells her truth and receives her friend's truth.

If we know a friend is speaking from her heart, we can honor her whether or not we agree. As a consequence we learn and grow from the differences between us. When friends have created a relationship with truth as a foundation, the respect that comes from that is more important than agreement.

Clara and Nancy, roommates and good friends, had standing plans to walk every Friday night. One Friday afternoon, Nancy heard Clara accept an invitation to go out with her new beau. Nancy was hurt that Clara, without even consulting her, had been so willing to ignore their plans. She spoke right out, saying she felt unimportant, definitely second-fiddle, and did not like being dropped for a man. Clara understood where she was coming from and apologized for hurting her. They are still best friends because they can tell each other the truth and are willing to hear each other's point of view even when they disagree.

～

After a whirlwind romance, Fran became engaged to a man her friend Simone knew was a womanizer. Simone warned her, and initially Fran resisted. However, Fran respected Simone and decided to postpone the wedding six months. During that time, the man showed his true colors, and Fran, heartbroken, ended the engagement. But she felt very grateful to Simone for telling her the truth.

∽

Pat invited Virginia, a single writer friend, to join her for a casual dinner with an out-of-town friend of Pat's, also a writer. At first, Virginia accepted, then called back and said she'd forgotten about a prior engagement. Pat sensed Virginia was lying and confronted her, saying, "It's O.K. with me if you've changed your mind and decided you don't want to come, but I know you don't have anything else to do. What bothers me is that you lied to me." Virginia quickly admitted to her lie, explaining she was feeling introverted and afraid to go out. Pat reassured her, Virginia went, and she had a great time. Virginia acknowledged the truth of her actions and what her friend had said to her, enabling the friendship to grow.

Truth furthers more truth, whereas lies beget lies. What happens if a friend responds to our openness and vulnerability by not being accountable, by pretending or denying she knows what we are talking about, or by twisting the situation so that we become at fault? Then an imbalance results and the friendship changes. We, as truth tellers, have to distance ourselves. It's impossible to be close friends with someone who lies, plays it safe, and keeps others at arm's length. As being true to ourselves and others becomes more and more essential, we want friends who feel the same way.

> Laurie told her friend Brenda, who had become a very heavy drinker, that she thought Brenda was ruining her health and her life. Brenda became furious, and so Laurie backed off and has never mentioned the problem again. Laurie realized that Brenda had low tolerance for hearing the truth.

～

> Clarissa's friend Edith went out and had a facelift and then never told her that she had had anything done. During the time Edith was recuperating, Clarissa tried to get together with her a few times, but there was always an excuse. When she finally saw Edith, she looked completely different from the last time they'd been together. Clarissa was so surprised she didn't know what to say, and she realized that Edith didn't want her to say a word. Edith acted as if nothing had happened. Clarissa felt very compromised having to perpetuate the charade, because what Clarissa wanted

in a close friend was someone who cared more about the interior than the facade.

~

Marion had been advised by her son's school to have him tutored, for they suspected he might have some learning differences. Because Tina had a background in education, Marion asked if Tina would tutor him. After a few sessions Tina came to the conclusion that the boy needed a more intensive program than Tina could offer and communicated that to Marion. This was clearly not what Marion had wanted to hear. After that Marion kept her distance, and their friendship definitely cooled. As a parent Tina understood how vulnerable we all are in regard to any issue concerning our children. But she had thought they were close enough friends that she could risk speaking honestly.

Whenever we feel a dissonance between what a friend is saying and what she is doing, we may have trouble staying committed to the friendship. We all enjoy friendly acquaintances, but in our real friendships, having them centered in the truth becomes the pivot point around which they thrive.

Heartfelt Advice
Helps a Friend in Need

I had a good lesson in the value of truth telling from a woman I've known since high school. Actually, she wasn't a close friend, but, as we still live in the town where we grew up, we got together occasionally. Being with her, however, became harder and harder for me as her life fell apart. She had three kids by three different men, none of whom she married. She didn't work regularly and was sometimes on welfare. She was also overweight, a heavy smoker, and seemed not to care at all about her appearance. Furthermore, when we saw each other, she did nothing but complain about her life. I never knew what to say to her and came to dread even running into her.

One day she called and asked if she could get my advice on finding a job. I was uneasy but agreed to see her. Mindful of her emotional state, I nonetheless decided to be straightforward with her and gave her what I thought were some useful, manageable suggestions on doing a resume, interviewing, and her appearance.

She responded negatively to everything I said with comments like "Oh, I can't do that" or "No one is going to talk to me about that job" or "You just don't understand how awful my life is." Despite the fact that she had asked me for advice, she was unable to get beyond her own self-pity. By the time we parted I felt a combination of anger with her for taking up my time, guilt that I hadn't handled it better, and pity for her. But I also felt good that I had spoken the truth from my heart. I decided that the next time I wouldn't agree to see her, and I would tell her why.

About six months later, I ran into her and could hardly believe my eyes. She looked twenty years younger. She had lost a lot of weight, her hair was neatly styled, and she was dressed well. Most of all she had a big smile on her face when she saw me. She gave me a big hug and started thanking me profusely. I was dumbstruck and couldn't imagine what she was thanking me for.

She apologized for being so negative the last time we'd seen each other and said that the last time we had talked, she was about at rock bottom. She went home contemplating suicide. She knew I was angry with her, and she hated the pity she saw on my face. But after a sleepless night, some of the things I said started resonating.

That very night, she took the first of what became nightly long walks when the kids were asleep. In addition to giving her time to think about her life, the walks helped her start losing weight. She asked a sister for some regular help with her kids and found a part-time job. While it didn't pay well, she was learning a lot and felt it was a good stepping stone for something better in the near future. She told me she had meant to call me for ages to thank me. Running into me that day was an answer to her prayer, for she felt that seeing, for me, would be believing.

It's a wonderful thing to know you have made a difference to someone, and, while I wish I had known earlier so that I wouldn't have felt so angry with her every time I thought about her, the smile on her face and the bounce in her step were a big enough reward to wipe out my memories of that last meeting between us and to convince me that I should never be afraid to speak the truth.

—KAREN, 53, LONG ISLAND, NY

Comment:

Truth telling is tricky. The teller, in any case, has to speak from her heart, and whether or not the friend is ready to hear it is up to the friend.

Speaking Up

A friend called me about a party for a mutual friend. My father, from whom I'd been estranged, had died since we last spoke. She hadn't called or written. When I mentioned how hard his death had been for me, she didn't respond. I said, "Kathy, I care about you and our friendship, and I hope you know that what I am going to say is coming from a place of love. I can't continue this conversation until I tell you that I am bummed you haven't said anything to me about Dad's dying." After a silence she said, "I thought you and your father hadn't spoken in a long time, and I really didn't know what to say."

There is no doubt that my father and I had difficulties, but his death put an end to any hope of reconciliation, to any chance of transformation in our relationship. I was grieving for what I yearned for in a father and never had as well as what now would never be.

I explained to Kathy how painful it feels, no matter what the circumstances, when someone loses a parent. I also said that when the relationship is a bitter, unresolved one some-times the death is harder to bear. At least in a loving one we know we were loved, and our love was accepted in return.

The bottom line is that a person is bereft when a friend averts her eyes and her heart, and is comforted when a friend reaches out and acknowledges the situation. A note as simple as "I know this must not be easy for you; I'm thinking of you" makes all the difference.

My friend Kathy apologized and thanked me for helping her see something she felt she should have understood. She thanked me, too, for teaching her a lesson as important as she considered this one to be—that of reaching out to anyone who is hurting and in need of loving human connection. We then talked awhile about my feelings of loss and sadness, and she lis-tened and empathized. I cannot tell you what a gift she gave me in being there so I could talk. She told me I'd given her a gift as well, and that next time (even if the situation is a compli-cated one) she will be there to hold a friend's hand.

I realize I had the choice to say nothing about my feeling disappointed in her silence and hence to harbor resentment, or I could talk to her about it. I decided to speak up because I care about myself, about her, and about our having an honest friend-ship. Rather than shut down on my negative feelings toward her and risk distancing myself from her, I chose to be truthful with her in the hope of enlarging our friendship. I know that some women would have reacted very differently, but I was lucky because Kathy responded in such a kind, healthy way. I cherish her now even more as my friend.

—LB

Comment:

When a friend is faced with difficulties, no matter what the circumstances, it is always better to say something than nothing. Even if what we say is that we are at a loss for words, at least we are acknowledging our friend's pain. Nothing means more to a friend at a time of loss than hearing expressions of caring and concern.

Something Only a Real Friend Would Do

My mother set great store by friendship, but she didn't always approve of my friends. She used to say obliquely, "Your best friend is the one who brings out the best in you." My friend Patty actually did that for me, but it wasn't fun. It was an unbearably painful experience. More than fifty years have gone by, but it still hurts to think about it.

I grew up on Army posts around the globe, the daughter of a colonel. My friends were "Army brats," with whom I had a lot in common. After graduation from Balboa High School in the Canal Zone, I sailed north on an army transport to go to college in New England. My father's parting words were "The most valuable part of college can be the 'education of friendship.'" I had no idea what he meant then, but I do now.

At Wellesley I discovered "friends" with whom I seemed to have nothing in common. Then in sophomore year, I met Patty—a turning point. Although she had been raised in a completely civilian world, we connected. What brought us together was golf. She belonged to a club in Cleveland, and Army bases always had golf courses. Our frequent golf games were always competitive, often hilarious.

We also took long canoe trips on the Charles River. Munching peanut butter sandwiches and sipping Coca-Cola from glass bottles, we discussed such topics as which man is better, the physical athlete or the mental athlete? Which band swings better, Glen Gray or Glenn Miller? Sometimes we read poetry aloud. Our favorite, naturally, was *The Rubáiyat of Omar Khayyám*:

A Book of Verses underneath the Bough,
A Jug of Wine, a Loaf of Bread—and Thou
Beside me singing in the Wilderness—
Oh, Wilderness were Paradise enow!

At that time I was in love with West Point. My older brother, Red Reeder, graduated from the Military Academy;

my sister married a West Point graduate; and they were all stationed at the Point. I went there to visit as often as possible. But not to see *them;* "Thou" for me meant cadets. I went to see the cadets—the more cadets, the better.

I also persuaded college friends, including Patty, to join me in enjoying the unlimited supply of cadets. I thought the U.S. Military Academy was the place to be and talked of little else. A friend would say, "How many cadets have you been out with this month?" Oblivious to the edge in her voice, I'd launch into a lengthy reply. If I left her glassy-eyed with boredom, I was unaware of it.

Blessed as I am now with 20/20 hindsight, I would say that I was as self-absorbed as I could get. Yet I had no idea that my conversation was limited to two topics, myself and the Corps of Cadets.

In our junior year Patty and I lived with a group of girls— as we were then called—in a dorm with a large tower suite. One evening I heard laughter exploding in the next room. The murmur of low voices would erupt into peals and shouts. Something was very, very funny. I paid no real attention, though the uproar continued a long time. I was packing to leave next day for the Army-Yale game.

Late that night Patty came into my room. She didn't say anything, she just stood there. Then she almost whispered, "Do you know what all the laughing was about?"

"I have no idea," I replied, snuggling under my gray West Point blanket.

"You," she said. "They were making fun of you."

I sat up straight. "That laughter was at me?"

Patty sat down on my bed. "They think you are nutty on West Point. They've all been swapping stories about your obsession and how easy it is to egg you on until you make a fool of yourself. I hate saying this, but I thought you ought to know about it." I spent the whole night crying.

When I opened my swollen eyes in the morning, I felt limp and forlorn. I didn't want to see anybody. I sent a telegram (those were the days) to my date saying I was sick, which I was. I could not bear to go to breakfast in the dorm. Putting on dark glasses, I walked to the village, head down, scuffing through dry leaves. My scrambled eggs in a little alley cafe tasted like cardboard.

A lonely weekend loomed ahead. I wasn't going to the game, and I wasn't going back to the tower suite. Where could I go to escape the humiliation? I grabbed the only lifeline available: I would throw myself into my studies. I decided to hide out in the library.

To my relief, there were few students in the marble sanctuary on that golden October Saturday. I had the place to myself. All semester I had been avoiding an art history paper on *Mont St. Michel and Chartres* by Henry Adams, heavy going. Now I would face it. I immersed myself in the assignment. During that long library weekend, a new world slowly opened before me. For the first time, really, I encountered the discipline and the joy of learning.

On Sunday morning I stopped working long enough to attend chapel. The preacher was the Reverend Charles O.

Taylor from Cambridge, and I have never forgotten his text. "Friendship," Dr. Taylor said, "is the elixir of life." That sent me scurrying back to the library to get a dictionary.

For the Greeks, I discovered, an elixir was a powder that dried wounds. For medieval alchemists, an elixir was a compound that would change base metal to gold. For us, an elixir is the quintessence—or refined spirit—of anything, a rare substance that gives you a lift.

I studied hard that weekend. When I began to lose track of what time it was, I knew I was on to something. I had come seeking refuge, but by Sunday night I was almost, not quite, "singing in the wilderness," only "thou" was now college itself.

Years later I found this passage in T. H. White's *The Once and Future King*: "The best thing for being sad," Merlin advised the despondent young Arthur, "is to learn something. . . . Learn why the world wags and what wags it. . . . Learning," Merlin said, "is the thing for you."

That autumn, as I gradually regained my self-esteem, I realized what the great lesson to come out of this shattering experience was. It was not just discovering the healing power of the life of the mind. It was discovering what it means to be a friend.

Patty did something only a real friend would do. She took the risk of telling me the awful truth. By leveling with me about the ridicule of "friends" she didn't exactly turn my life to gold, but she did turn me around. My mother always told me that I talked too much. "Ask, don't tell," she would say. Now for the first time, I heard her. I began to try focusing on others instead of myself.

Now I know that my father's "education of friendship" has a two-way stretch. Since I had never discussed these appalling events with Patty, I decided to send the story to her in California. She wrote back, "Your letter was a total surprise. I never dreamed I had any impact on your life. Thanks for telling me. I've just had a cancer operation and you gave me a much-needed lift."

Friendship really is the elixir of life.

—NARDI REEDER CAMPION, 81, HANOVER, NH

Comment:
When the motive for telling the truth comes from a clear and loving place, even the most difficult message can make a big difference.

A Banker for Friends

Lending money to friends can be tricky, and it seems to be my karma to do it over and over. Not that I am rich by any means; I am just richer than these borrower friends and, I guess, a soft touch. To me the important thing about lending money to a friend is making repayment terms clear between you. Either the money changing hands is a loan and should be repaid on an agreed-to schedule, or it is a gift and should be acknowledged by both parties as such. It is loans that turn into unintended gifts that are a problem between friends.

I have a friend I have lent money to numerous times over the past twenty years. Some of it she has repaid and some she hasn't—yet. The owed amounts are tied to the day her ship comes in. As to the other amounts, it is almost as though she has a revolving line of credit with me.

Recently she asked if she could borrow $1,000—again. First, I made it clear that the money had to be repaid and quite quickly. We settled on a repayment schedule of $200 per month. The first check arrived about on time. The second check was late, but she called to tell me things were slower than she had expected, and asked if she could delay repaying the rest. I said I would rather get less per month than get nothing at all, so we settled on $100 per month. After that, a check arrived every month until the loan was repaid. We are currently on another round of repayments on that revolving $1,000.

I wish for her sake that it wasn't necessary for her to keep borrowing money. However, I am glad I can be there for her in this way, and I know our friendship has lasted through all of this "thick and thin" because we have been open about the terms of the loans. Her being accountable for the money means our friendship can go on unaffected by our long-standing lender-borrower relationship, and I know we both look forward to the day when neither one of us is a borrower or a lender, to paraphrase Shakespeare.

—MK

> ### *Comment:*
> When there are money issues between friends, it is vital to be clear, honest, and accountable.

A Grifter

I took a class on film recently, and we discussed *The Grifters*, a movie about predatory people who take advantage of innocent ones. It showed how easily we can get into trouble when we put on blinders and decide not to see certain things, when we are willfully naive. All of us, to a certain point, want to be seduced by the fantasy of goodness, but if we never look at the dark side of life, we blind ourselves and become susceptible to great danger. The longer we repress anything unpleasant or upsetting, the easier it is to betray ourselves or be betrayed by someone else.

This movie clarified for me how perpetrators will do anything to get their way, and that unless someone steps in and stops them, they will keep on being destructive. I saw it at an opportune time because I was having problems with a "friend." It helped me understand certain negative aspects of friendship and also validated a stand I took with her, a stand that caused the friendship to end.

We were mothers together. Our sons met in preschool and were great friends. They played well, enjoyed similar interests, and I was happy that Matt had such a nice playmate. Joan did things, however, from time to time that made me feel uneasy.

She'd pretend she hadn't said something when she had. She wouldn't "understand" if her son did anything wrong. She wouldn't follow any rules except her own. But I put on blinders and let her behavior slide because it wasn't affecting my son and because I knew she wouldn't listen. Both boys went on to the same kindergarten; all went well for a few years, until I noticed a dynamic developing that was beginning to affect my son in an adverse way.

Joan initiated a not-so-subtle campaign to undermine and ostracize Matt (I now understand that she perceived him to be too much competition for her son), and he was becoming confused and unhappy. Part of what was making her so dangerous was that she was using her son for her own agenda. Since she and her son were powerful and charismatic, they were successful in recruiting kids to their side. Initially, I watched, not quite knowing what I could do. Then one day I heard that Joan was applying for her son to become a member of a club where my son and I belong.

Since I was one of the few members Joan knew well, the normal course of action would have been for her to ask me for help, but she didn't. Instead she bypassed me. I suppose she thought she could power her way in without having to be accountable or change her behavior toward my son in any way.

I realized that here was a place I had some power and I should use it, for I understood (finally) that people like Joan stop and listen only to someone who has worldly power equal to them and who is willing to use it. After talking with her sponsor and explaining the situation, I called Joan and suggested she wait to apply for membership for her son until we could sort out our differences. At first she played dumb and pretended she had no idea what I was talking about, either to do with joining the club or with any problems. But when I tried to pin her down and force her to acknowledge her actions, she flew into a rage and hasn't talked to me since.

After I challenged her to be accountable, after I let her know I would no longer tolerate her abusive behavior, she and her son backed off from mine, and the polarization and competitive behavior that had been escalating in their class stopped. My son wasn't old enough to stand up to both Joan and her son, but he saw me say "Stop, no more" to Joan. We both learned how important it is in our relationships to stand up to people who are abusing power, to stop them in their tracks before they do irreversible damage.

—JESSICA, 38, NEW YORK CITY

Comment:

Sometimes we absolutely must challenge a "friend" who is not being truthful and accountable, because if we don't, we risk losing ourselves to an unhealthy relationship. Being truthful empowers us regardless of the repercussions.

The Bottom Line

A single woman I was "growing" a friendship with told me over tea one afternoon that she was contemplating having an affair with a married man, someone she had been working with. The problem was that I knew the man—and his wife—and had been friends of theirs for years.

The woman claimed that the man told her his wife sanctioned his occasional liaisons. But I knew how terribly hurt the wife was by his behavior. Nonetheless, I remained silent. Maybe I was too stunned to react. She went on about how she wasn't looking for a long-term relationship; she just wanted a fun fling. I managed to say that I thought she should really think about it more first.

However, the more I thought about it after she left, the worse I felt. I decided I had to tell her how I really felt, which was that she was espousing values I didn't relate to at all. I could never knowingly hurt another woman like that, even if I didn't know her. And this woman had met the wife. While she didn't know that I knew the wife's true feelings about her husband's indiscretions, she was clearly choosing her own selfish desires over the wife's feelings.

I called her. We had a difficult conversation and she reacted with surprise to my views. By the end I had decided that I could never cultivate a friendship with this woman, whose values were so different from my own. Since that conversation, we haven't really been in touch, which is fine with me. I am glad I spoke my mind to her and just hope I gave her food for thought.

—Cynthia, 46, Miami

Comment:

We all have a wide variety of friendships that serve us in different, important ways. In each of these friendships, there are varying degrees of closeness, depending on how willing we are to speak the truth to each other. For real intimacy, we have to be true to ourselves, speaking the truth from our hearts.

A Facade

What I need in a close friend is for that person to be true to herself. If she isn't, I have a big problem maintaining that friendship. I had a friend who was denying who she was. I tried to talk to her, but I couldn't get past her barriers. She resented my probing, and I was frustrated because I couldn't get through to her core. We are not friends anymore.

I have learned this through my own experience. Once I had a boyfriend who wanted me to be different than I was. He told me to be more extroverted, to become more the take-charge type. I adapted to his demands. My two sisters were upset with me. I tried rationalizing with them, saying "But I'm still who I am with you." They responded with "That's not enough. You need to be who you are consistently in your life."

What they were saying rang true to me because I was feeling depressed and uncomfortable with myself. When I stopped trying to act like someone else, my boyfriend left. But I am very grateful to my sisters for challenging me and for helping me to strip away my facade.

I came away from this situation knowing that I never wanted to be who I am not. When I see someone who pretends, I keep my distance. By the way, my two sisters are my closest friends. I know they speak the truth, and they expect the same from me. I also know they will never run away from who they are.

—KRIS, 26, LOS ANGELES

Comment:
When we are true to ourselves we can speak the truth with integrity to others.

The Truth Sets Us Free

Keeping secrets divides us from ourselves and from each other. I know from experience. It used to be very hard for me to reveal to a friend any flaws or painful parts of my life. For example, I never graduated from college, and I had always been embarrassed that I didn't have a college degree. Whenever someone talked of their academic career, I managed to divert the conversation away from me.

One day I was with my close friend Leslie, a Stanford graduate. She was reminiscing about her college days. Because I valued our friendship and wanted to become closer to her, I decided to take a risk. I took a deep breath and said, "Leslie, I only have a high school diploma." She turned to me and answered, "Sara, sometimes degrees and labels can get in the way of what is real and important. You are one of the wisest women I know. Don't ever forget that."

As soon as I'd told her what I'd been so ashamed of, what I'd been hiding for so long, the power of my secret was diffused. And when she received it in such a respectful and loving way, our friendship was strengthened. Since then Leslie has shared some pretty painful parts of herself with me as well, and our friendship has expanded.

I have another friend, Patty, who always paints a perfect picture of her life. I know from others that her mother has tried to commit suicide many times, but Patty has never once confided in me. Instead she maintains a strong front. She simply cannot open up and share anything intimate with me. This makes it difficult for us to be close in any meaningful way.

I know now that every time I tell my truth to my close friend and she responds in kind, our bond of friendship deepens.

—SARA, 48, ST. LOUIS, MO

No Chance for Good-Bye

Two years ago, one of my best childhood friends died of ovarian cancer. I never got the chance to see her and say good-bye
because she didn't tell me she was dying. In fact, I didn't even
know she had cancer until her mother called me to tell me she
had died.

I was terribly upset and found myself feeling very angry
with her and then feeling guilty for feeling angry, even though
I was told by her mother that by the time she was diagnosed, it
was only a few weeks till she died. One day I started crying as I
was talking with a friend about Sara's death, and she suggested
I write Sara a letter and tell her all the things I hadn't had the
chance to tell her. At first I felt uncomfortable, but I just went
ahead and did it. I told her how much I loved her and missed
her. I told her how angry I was with her for not confiding in me
(and others close to her). I told her that I knew she must have
been in a state of shock and denial about her illness, but that I

still thought it was unfair, even mean, that she kept the news to herself and didn't let me express my love for her. I couldn't help feeling that she didn't care about me because it was really an unloving thing for her to do. I told her about the pain I was in and how left out I felt. Five pages later I was still writing.

I can't really explain it, but it did make me feel better. I like to believe I learned a lesson from her sad death and feel I would behave differently with my loved ones were I to find myself in her place. After all, I want to be remembered lovingly and kindly and, after this experience, I am convinced we must die truthfully as well as live truthfully with others.

—ANDREA, 43, AUSTIN, TX

Comment:

Everyone chooses her own way of dying, but withholding that truth from our loving friends is hurtful. It denies us the opportunity to express our feelings and say good-bye. But out of loss we learn lessons of how we want to communicate with others.

When a Lie Is Best

When I was seventeen, my stepfather of many years—a very successful and well-known man in his field but extremely moody, selfish, and demanding at home—put the moves on my best friend when she was visiting us. Very upset, she immediately told me what had happened, as we hid nothing from each other. At first, I was so stunned and disgusted that I didn't want to believe her. But she was not one to lie or even embellish, and it was obvious she was telling the truth. Her experience also rang true with me because I had had my suspicions for some time that he was not faithful to my mom, although she was totally devoted to him.

Even now I don't know how I found the courage, but I confronted him about it. He became furious. He yelled at me and called me a liar and worse. His anger was enough to convince me that he knew I had caught him red-handed. Still, I decided then and there that I wasn't going to tell my mother. A few years earlier, she had had a nervous breakdown, and I felt she was too fragile to handle this latest event. I also knew things would never be the same at home.

Sure enough, practically the day I turned eighteen, he kicked me out of the house. Basically, he told my mother it was either him or me, and she chose him. He never gave her any explanation other than to say I was impossible to have around. He just couldn't stand it that I knew what a snake he really was. I was hurt, of course, that she chose him over me, but I understood it based on her own needs. Besides, I was really ready to get out. My only regret was that I couldn't take her with me. They have since divorced, and she now knows what really happened. I still feel I was being her friend by not telling her. She, in fact, recently told me she agrees with me.

—PAM, 36, HOUSTON

Fair-Weather Friend

I'm an actress, and for a while I was very friendly with my agent. Being in the same industry, we had lots of common interests, so we went to the theater, saw movies, and had long dinners discussing show business. We enjoyed each other's company a lot. She also worked hard to get me put up for parts.

Our friendship developed during the first six months of a one-year contract I had with her firm. During that period, unfortunately, not a lot of work came my way. This meant, of course, that her firm wasn't earning much money from me because agents earn 10 percent of what their clients earn.

Gradually, I noticed a change in her attitude toward me. She stopped initiating things for us to do, and when I suggested something she either had an excuse or she would agree to it and then cancel at the last moment. She made references to other clients whose careers were taking off or very busy, especially women of my age and "type." Once, I remember, she invited me to a client's concert, then discouraged me from going backstage with her after the show. She made it seem as though I wasn't important enough. I felt increasingly uneasy around her, and despite several attempts on my part to check in with her about what was going on, she never told me.

Finally, as the end of the year approached, she uneasily told me the firm wasn't going to represent me anymore. I was hurt, disappointed, and also angry with her for not being honest with me all along. She had been afraid to tell me about her firm's disappointment in my performance. Instead, I got no warning except what my intuition was telling me. We tried to get together a few times after I left the agency, but I was uncomfortable and so was she. I didn't feel I could trust her to be honest with me, and I think she felt guilty about how she had handled the situation. I definitely need my friends to tell me the truth and take responsibility for their actions.

—LIZ, 40, LOS ANGELES

Comment:

Whether or not there is a power imbalance between us, when a work relationship edges into a friendship, the truth becomes even more critical, for holding back information can cause repercussions that damage both the work relationship and the friendship. Consciously establishing truthful boundaries and guidelines helps create a clear understanding.

Keeping Things Clear

Mary invited me over the other evening to watch a rough cut of a movie she was interested in supporting. She had seen it once already, was enthusiastic about its future success, and wanted my opinion. While I am nowhere near as qualified as Mary is in judging a movie's merits, I was honored she'd asked me to look at it.

I knew I was seeing the movie at its worst (tiny screen, scenes left out and ending incomplete, voices dubbed, sound unclear), and so I tried hard to visualize it in its final form. But even overlooking all that, I was not very touched by it. For me, the plot was confusing and hard to follow, some of the characters and their motivations were blurred, and I was not caught up in the emotional drama of the story.

Having already produced one movie and viewed many more than I ever have, Mary has a lot of history and expertise in this field. Aware of my lack of credentials, I was somewhat hesitant to express my opinion, but I knew she wanted my honest evaluation. I told her that I thought the movie was courageous and interesting, but that I was surprisingly unmoved by it.

While I think Mary was disappointed that I was not as excited about it as she was, I know she appreciated my honesty. She told me later that she was glad I had trusted our friendship enough to take this risk. She added that had I said I'd loved the movie, she would have asked me to help her raise some money for it.

Then I would have been faced with a dilemma. How could I have asked other people to support a project that my heart wasn't in? It would have been very difficult for me. More difficult than that, however, would have been the fact that I hadn't been straightforward with Mary right from the start.

—LB

Comment:

Unless there are some compelling reasons not to, it is always best to be truthful with friends. The more we choose to tell the truth, the better able we are to be clear with ourselves and our friends, thus honoring the true essence of friendship.

Learning a Lesson about Truth

Sometimes it's what we don't tell a friend that is important. I lost a friend over what I didn't tell her.

Years ago, I worked with a woman who became quite a good friend. She and I usually had lunch once a week, and my husband and I saw her and her husband socially.

Initially secondhand, and then through direct observation, I learned that her husband was having an affair with a woman we both knew. Because I felt it wasn't really my "place" to get involved in her marriage, I didn't tell my friend. Eventually, of course, she found out what was going on. She brought it up, and I told her I had known. She was furious, and from then until I moved away, she kept her distance.

In hindsight, I believe I made a big mistake by not telling her. I'm not sure if this particular issue can ever be black or white, but in this case, I misjudged her. She wanted to hear the truth from a friend. She didn't like the fact that I had known something so important about her life and had kept it from her. I guess I was afraid she'd shoot the messenger. Instead, I got shot for not being a messenger.

I haven't run into this situation again, but if I do, I will opt for the truth. If I am told to mind my own business, so be it, but better to lose a friend because she can't handle the truth than to lose a friend because I can't.

—RITA, 50, BURLINGTON, VT

Comment:

It's important to know our friends and to know what our friends want. Some friends want to hear the truth under any circumstance; others don't. We have to be clear about any friend's need for the truth. Our desire to be in friendship with someone whose tolerance for the truth—either hearing it or speaking it—is much less than our own is another matter and inevitably influences the quality of the friendship.

FIVE

~

Trust in Friendships

*W*ithout trust, close friendships cannot survive. In order to trust, we need to feel safe with a friend. Can we be open and vulnerable with her and feel that she will not hurt us? Can we ask her for help? Will she keep our confidences?

Building a friendship based on trust doesn't happen overnight; rather it evolves over time. We test the waters by taking a risk, in being vulnerable and sharing some intimate detail about ourselves. Or we ask for help or reveal a hurt. When a friend's response validates the trust we've placed in her, when she honors our story or gives her help freely, the friendship strengthens out of the sense of safety we feel.

Positive experiences encourage us to be more vulnerable, more open, and we share more of who we really are. We speak about our hopes, dreams, beliefs, fears, and past experiences. Our friend responds in kind, and the friendship grows and deepens. Each of us is entrusting a part of herself to the other. There is a back and forth movement of risking, trusting, then risking and trusting again, like stepping stones between friends.

Maria and Laura, close friends, had coffee after seeing *Il Postino*. They talked about how they both loved the scene when the postman talks to Neruda on the beach about metaphors. Suddenly, Maria began to cry, and Laura quickly followed suit. When the waiter rushed over with two fresh napkins, they looked at each other and dissolved into laughter. Even in a public place, they felt completely safe with each other.

Tina tearfully told Abbey that she had been abused by her father as a child. She had felt so ashamed that she had never told anyone before. Her willingness to trust her friend despite her fear that Abbey would turn against her drew them closer together. Abbey felt honored that Tina trusted her enough, and their friendship deepened.

There will, of course, be disagreements; waters won't always be calm. None of us acts perfectly all the time. However, most of the time we try hard to be a trustworthy friend, and if we breach this trust, we make amends as best we can. We are wiser as a result, and with accountability, we are able to forgive and move forward.

Friendships falter, however, when we abuse our power by lying, betraying confidences, or using a friend for personal gain and then refusing to acknowledge our hurtful acts. Trust is violated when a friend lies and pretends she didn't, or when she selectively remembers and then walks away when challenged to be truthful and accountable. Trust is also compromised when someone betrays a friend by telling her secrets or using them later as a weapon to hurt her; or when she uses her friend because of something she wants—social position, her husband, money, her friends, or advantages for her children—and then turns her back when she no longer needs her.

Cynthia's good friend Sara, who was having marital problems, sat next to Cynthia's husband at a dinner party. Sara told Tom untrue things about how Cynthia felt about Cynthia's marriage. Tom was so upset that he and Cynthia left right after dinner was over, and he told her why on their way home. Cynthia was stunned. She realized Sara was trying to chip away at her marriage. Cynthia felt betrayed, and she no longer trusted Sara.

~

Bettina fell leaving a restaurant. Marcie, jealous of her friend's success in her job, spread a rumor that Bettina was an alcoholic. When Bettina heard about the story and its source, she confronted Marcie. Marcie laughed and shrugged it off. After that Marcie avoided Bettina and gave others the impression that their friendship had ended because of something Marcie had done.

Anyone who behaves like this does not value the concept of trust and is not capable of being a reliable friend. She values getting ahead in the world more than the rewards of an intimate friendship based on trust. Given the choice, she will opt for the world of opportunity, money, and power over her friendship. These actions compromise and hurt the friend who values trust.

When we see our friend making these choices, we start to feel unsafe, and to protect ourselves, we move away from the friendship. Without trust as the foundation, it is impossible to build true intimacy in any friendship. As many of the following stories show, breaches of trust inevitably change the dynamics of the friendship. However, these difficult experiences test our values and provide us with the opportunity to learn valuable lessons about how important trust in friendship is.

Seeing Clearly

My son had just started going to a new school, and Carolyn's son was in his class. What I noticed first about her was her thick eyeglasses. She, like me, is extremely nearsighted. Having been in progressively thicker lenses since I was seven, I am highly tuned in to others' eyesight.

Luckily, I have successfully worn contacts since I was sixteen, but I still have to have a pair of glasses handy. Years ago an optician explained to me the "small and round" theory of eyeglasses when I was complaining about how much I hated my glasses with their thick lenses. For very myopic people, she said, the smaller and rounder the lens, the less thick the edges are. Therefore, the "coke bottle" effect I had always hated so much is minimized.

When I met her, Carolyn was wearing a large pair of rectangular-shaped glasses with very thick lenses. They were not flattering in any way. I could barely see her beautiful blue eyes. When she told me that she had stopped wearing contacts because of an eye infection, I decided to take a chance, trusting that Carolyn would take my comments as being as well meaning as they were intended. I suggested that if she were going to have to wear glasses for a while, perhaps she should consider getting a pair that was more flattering.

My comment was like throwing a lifeline to a drowning woman. She had been feeling awful about the way she looked and responded enthusiastically and hopefully when I told her about the small and round theory. I had just found an optician in town with an extensive frame selection who not only knew the theory but had told me about a new lens glass that enabled the lenses to be even thinner. I wanted to replace my existing lenses with the new, thinner lens and offered to take Carolyn with me and help her pick out new frames as well. My best friend always went with me, and I thought Carolyn might appreciate the same help. She was thrilled with the offer. We made a date for glasses and coffee a few days later. I even called the shop and made an appointment.

We spent several hours trying on glasses and talking to the optician about options. Carolyn found a very flattering pair, and I ordered the new lenses for my frames. We had a good time and became better acquainted, sharing our common fate of being "blind as a bat."

Out of my trusting her to respond positively, we went a long way toward building a friendship that day. I was as thrilled to help her as she was to have me help. I'm so glad I overcame any concern I might have had about hurting her feelings or being too bold. But since I had stood in her shoes, she trusted that I was coming from a kind place when I made the overture. Because of this good start, we've had many more opportunities to build up the trust between us.

—MK

Comment:
How we take that first small step toward each other sets the framework for a trusting friendship.

End of a Friendship

I've had one terrible experience with a friend. It happened over a disagreement about parenting. I know this is a place where we are very vulnerable, whether we choose to admit it or not. My husband and I and our three-year-old son were visiting my close friend and her husband. They had a son the same age as ours. Our sons indulged in a sort of minor sexual exploration, which we took with a grain of salt, realizing that this was not unusual for children of this age. My friend, however, went ballistic. Her reaction was way out of proportion to the actions of our three-year-olds.

My friend is inhibited. In the past we've had conversations about her feelings about sex. Her son's behavior brought up many of her issues, which at that time she hadn't resolved. Rather than acknowledging her own anxiety, she instead blamed me for what had happened. For a while I allowed her to do this because I didn't want to lose her as my friend. I just flipped onto my back and momentarily lost my sense of self. As long as she could scapegoat me and not look inside herself, our friendship was kept alive. I could feel it eroding, but I didn't want to let it go.

Because I was in so much pain over this, I finally went to a therapist, who assured me that my friend was completely out of line and that what our sons did was normal for three-year-olds. Right then I made the courageous decision to stop acting like the guilty party my friend could blame. As soon as my behavior shifted, and as soon as she realized she might have to be responsible, she then turned her back on me. Her reaction was total silence.

She was absolutely unwilling to look at anything beyond what was safe for her to see, beyond what she needed to believe. I was sad because it seemed as if our friendship was over, but I learned from this experience that when lack of accountability has a stronger pull than mutuality and growth, then it is not a healthy friendship.

I need my close friends to be willing, as I am, to risk looking deeper into themselves, to go to places that are difficult for us. For me, friends I trust help me go there safely to learn what I need to learn. They may learn something valuable as well.

—LISA, 32, NEW YORK CITY

P.S. Since I was interviewed, my friend called me up and apologized. She had done a lot of work and understood herself in a new way, as did I. And together we renewed our friendship and built an even stronger bridge of trust.

Comment:

Trust is one of the cornerstones of intimate friendship. To trust is to make ourselves vulnerable to another. Therefore, we need to feel safe enough to share our most intimate feelings and to know they will be heard and honored. If a friend is silent, if a friend walks away, if a friend denies any wrongdoing on her part—all these actions violate trust. As we grow within our friendships, we entrust our very selves to our friends. We become, in essence, each other's custodians. As custodians, we are accountable—that is, we accept our whole nature, including our shadow parts—and we need our friends to be accountable as well.

Safety First

I tend to be a risk taker when it comes to making new friends. Most of the time, my judgment is pretty good, but occasionally I make a mistake about whom I can trust. The mother of one of my son's classmates is a therapist. Having had a very positive experience with a therapist in my own life, I was inclined to trust her. I guess I assumed that anyone who had gone through all that psychologists go through to become trained would be pretty together.

Over a period of months, we spent time together because our sons played after school. I found myself opening up to her about certain things in my life having to do with my marriage. I even told her my husband had had an affair. As her own marriage was foundering, she was very vocal about how she felt about her husband. If I told her something about my husband, she would quote some book about dysfunctional marriages, putting my marriage in the same boat as hers.

At first, I thought she was just trying to be helpful, but I soon realized she was using my stories to fuel her own bitterness toward her husband. I think she was trying to get me to join her as a discontented wife, which I didn't feel I needed to do. I'm not implying I have a perfect marriage. However, I know my husband and I care about each other a lot and are willing to work at our relationship to keep it strong.

Because she was so willing to use my stories for her own purposes, I stopped confiding in her. I felt she was violating the trust I had placed in her. Over the next couple of years, our sons stopped being friends, and so did we. I just didn't feel safe with her.

—ERICA, 42, SEATTLE

Comment:

Inevitably we learn whom we can trust by placing our trust in someone we consider a friend. Sometimes we learn the hard way that we made the wrong choice. This lesson teaches us to be more aware of who we are and what we expect from our close friends.

Don't Hedge Your Bets

I don't have an answer for what is the right way to be a friend and what is the wrong way. I just want to tell you a story about friendship and let you come to your own conclusions. Sally and I have been really good friends for over twenty-five years, long before I was "lucky" enough to have a stepmother. When my father remarried, she was well aware of how difficult the situation became. She saw how Alice, my stepmother, came into my family and then ripped it to shreds. She watched Alice undermine me any chance she got. Sally and I had many conversations about what a manipulator and really harmful person Alice has been and is to me. She knows of the pain I've felt and has seen firsthand the tears I've shed over the fact that, through

Alice's campaigning, I, who was once my father's favorite, became the black sheep of the family.

My stepmother is interested only in money and social position. Recently, my father died and left all his money to her, and Alice couldn't wait to tell everyone in Houston that she "got it all." Alice is not a nice person; rather, the nicest adjective anyone can think of to describe her is "user friendly." But people court her anyway; the promise of being included in (or excluded from) her many parties is very seductive, and many women I know do not want to run the risk of getting on her bad side. Besides, now she has a lot of money and more power.

Sally and I got together recently, and our conversation turned to Alice. I talked of my feelings of hurt and loss and fully expected that my friend would empathize as usual and validate my feelings about my stepmother. Instead, she turned to me and said, "Just because you have problems with Alice, it doesn't concern me. She's always been pleasant and has never done anything to me. I don't have a problem with her. Besides, I don't want to make an enemy of her. Life is too short for that." I was shocked and didn't know what to say in response. Instead I changed the subject. When I was at home later with my husband, I told him what she'd said and how lonely and hurt I had felt by her words.

My husband comforted me and said, "I know that if the tables were turned, if you were in Sally's place, you would never hedge your bets like that." He's right; instead I'd say, "Sally, I don't know how anyone can have anything to do with that bitch; I never would, knowing how much she has hurt you. I care about our friendship much more than whether or not I go to any of Alice's parties." Unfortunately, I think I'm in a minority. I think many women would chastise me for wanting to control Sally's choice of friends. I think they'd agree with her.

In my opinion, everything, especially our values, has become too relative. We're afraid to take stands, to be consciously loyal, to stick our neck out in any way. Instead we choose to straddle the fence and be everyone's friend in hopes of not missing out on anything. I think when we act this way, we miss out on a lot, namely true, kind, intimate friendships.

—CHRISTINA, 38, HOUSTON

Comment:

When trust between friends is broken, we are very hurt in the process. It's hard to accept choices a friend makes that breach our trust, as this compromises the friendship. However, from painful experiences come important lessons that help us clarify fundamental values we want in our close friendships. When a friend's behavior challenges our values, we see more clearly what we expect from ourselves and our friends, and we endeavor to bring this greater wisdom to our existing and future friendships.

Will You Be My Friend?

I have not had many positive experiences with women being my real friends. Right now I am surrounded by people who might appear to be my friends, but that is because I'm married to a rich man, I give great parties, I donate to many charities, and I serve in powerful positions on several boards in this city. I am the flame that the moths flutter around. If I should stop giving parties or if I should lose my money or get divorced (or even widowed), then I'd become a liability, and very few of the women I know would stand by me and be trustworthy. They base their "friendships" on convenience—make no demands, and the "friendship" works.

Years ago, when I was divorcing my first husband, I learned the hard way about friends. At that time I had several friends whom I considered to be close, and I went to one of them and poured my heart out to her. I told her of my distress and my anxiety about being the one to leave my husband and how upset and uncertain I was about everything in my life. She sat there looking at me, and when I was finished, she said, "I don't believe you."

I was devastated, for I had really shared such a vulnerable part of me. Soon thereafter, I heard she was entertaining my estranged husband, a real mover and shaker in town. When he got engaged, this "friend" was part of the wedding party. I went to her and said, "You don't even know Joan; how can you be her bridesmaid? I thought you were *my* friend." And she simply replied, "Oh, Joan's a lot of fun."

When you get a divorce, even if you are the one leaving, even if you have another man waiting for you, you don't hurt any less than the one who is left. It's an incredibly sad, difficult time, especially if there are children involved. For a long time I agonized over whether I was doing the right thing or not. The women I thought were my friends never once acknowledged my pain. Instead, they all rallied around my husband. When he remarried, they gave parties for him and his new wife.

Then when I remarried and they saw that my new husband had money and power, they came flocking back to my side. I ask myself sometimes why I invite these people to my parties, but if I excluded everyone who had burned me, I'd have no one to invite! I just don't expect anything very much from my women friends except a fair-weather friendship.

I belong to an exercise group, but we talk mainly about professional things. It's a good place to let off some steam but on a very superficial level. Once I shared with them a story about my husband's daughter (who is very mixed up), and they didn't believe me. Later they found out from someone else that what I'd said was absolutely true. I had let down my guard a little, but after this I learned never to show them any chinks in my armor again. I know they like my husband better than they like me, and if I ever got divorced again, they would befriend him and drop me. It is terrible when you have no friends.

When I was going through my divorce, I saw a therapist for a while, and she zeroed in on this issue of lack of friendship. She said to me straight out that the one tremendous deficit in my life was that I did not have any friends I could really trust, and that one day I'd be alone and that I would need friends. I think about what she said a lot, and when I go to a party, I look around and wonder, Could anyone here be my friend? Thank God I'm married to my best friend and that my children are trusted friends as well.

—MARGARET, 49, DALLAS, TX

Comment:
Even if we've been hurt in friendship, it is important to keep looking for opportunities to make new, trusted friends. A life without friends is a lonely one.

Learning the Hard Way

A college incident from over twenty years ago involving my then best friend came back into sharp focus a few weeks ago when my husband and I had dinner with her. As the evening progressed, I became increasingly uncomfortable because she was very obviously flirting with him.

Our junior year, Tricia and I roomed together. It was great living with my best friend. We talked about everything, including the men in our lives. She knew all about the flirtation I was having with this radical school leader, for instance.

One evening, the phone rang and Tricia answered it. Her voice got real low. She took the phone into her bedroom and closed the door, an unprecedented move in our house. A few minutes later, she came out of the room, grabbed her bike, and left without a word.

I had agreed to meet Mr. Radical at his apartment the next morning. When I pulled up in front of his building, there was Tricia's bike leaning by his front door. Stunned, I left immediately, feeling totally betrayed.

Quite frankly, I barely spoke to her for the rest of the school year. While we never openly talked about it, she knew that I knew what had happened.

Since we live in the same city, I have seen her off and on over the years, and I'm sorry to say I've heard stories about her from others echoing my own experience. Occasionally I wondered if I had been too hard on her or if I should be a bigger person and put the past behind us. Perhaps it was out of those feelings of largesse that the recent dinner took place. Her behavior that evening, substantiated by my husband later, only confirmed that she's still no friend of mine. If I can't trust a woman, I can't count her as a friend. Trust is the bottom line for me.

—CAROLYN, 44, DETROIT

Comment:

If the betrayer acknowledges her actions and makes amends, we can keep our hearts open to trust again. However, if the betrayer is not accountable, real trusting friendship necessarily ends. But the person betrayed is wiser and stronger because she knows from the hurtful experience how important trust is to her.

The High Price of Decorating

Ten years ago my husband and I moved to a new city. I was excited because one of my close childhood friends, Kathy, also lived there now. We quickly recaptured the intimacy we'd had before. I was having some marital problems and subsequently suspected that my husband had begun an affair. I confided in Kathy, telling her of my anxiety and pain. She was great. She listened, commiserated, held my hand, and when my fears were confirmed, she was upset. Or at least she told me she was upset.

While she was only an acquaintance of Kathy's, the "other woman" happened to know many of the women Kathy ran around with. This other woman had a lot of money and gathered people around her. I see now the reasons why so many women courted her: she could offer them fun parties, good presents, and a sense of being part of the "in-group."

My husband ultimately ended the affair, and our marriage continued, but I was very hurt. Kathy knew of my deep feelings; I told her many times how betrayed I felt. A few years later, my marriage ended. While I know that the affair was only a reaction to other problems that existed between my husband and me, nevertheless, it left a permanent mark on my soul. I felt publicly humiliated, very lonely and alone.

At the time Kathy sympathized, saying that she, too, would have felt exactly the same way. I naively thought that she, my close friend, would always stand by my side. Was I ever wrong! Recently, another friend told me she'd heard that Kathy, who is an interior decorator, had just accepted a job to redo the house of the woman who'd had the affair with my husband. I told that person that she must have gotten the wrong information.

I immediately called Kathy and left a message for her to call. Two days went by. I called again and left another message. The third time I called, she answered. I asked her if what I'd heard was true, and she said it was. I felt sick inside. How could she accept a job, a job she did for fun and not because she needed the business or the money, that would put her in such a close and friendly position with this woman? I told Kathy that not only was I hurt but that I felt she was giving out the wrong message.

I explained what I meant by that. I said that if we were the close friends that everyone considered us to be, then her accepting that particular decorating job was undermining our friendship. By her actions Kathy was telling the world that she was happy to be helping out and working with the very person who'd had a long, messy affair with my then husband. In accepting that job, Kathy was choosing not to address what had happened, and I felt she was compromising our friendship.

Kathy dismissed my feelings, saying that since the affair was long past, I should get on with my life. She was offended that I had challenged her and said I should "grow up." Her response really hurt me. I tried unsuccessfully several times to talk it out with her, and now she avoids me when she can. She's also begun gathering around her friends we've shared together, and I am being left more and more out of the group. Suddenly it seems as if what happened is all my fault.

Am I right or wrong in expecting Kathy to be more loyal to me? Is it fair to ask a close friend to act in the way I wanted Kathy to, or am I being unreasonable? I'm confused, but in my heart of hearts, I'm pretty sad because I don't feel Kathy and I will ever be as close as we were before.

She had other choices—she could have graciously declined the assignment, she could even have expressed surprise that the woman had dared ask her, knowing what close friends the two of us were, or she could have acknowledged that she'd hurt me and apologized.

For me it's important to be loyal and to stand by a friend; Kathy played both sides, choosing the convenient way out. By doing so, she breached the trust in our friendship. Things between us will never be the same. She hurt me, but I believe she hurt herself the most.

—HILARY, 38, TAMPA, FL

Comment:

Being loyal to our friends is intrinsic to close friendship. Especially in times of need, we remember those sturdy, stand-by-me friends who help us keep going. We are confronted daily with choices, and every time we choose to be loyal to our friends, we help them, and ourselves, as well.

Losing a Mentor

I am a landscape architect. I love my work and have been fortunate to have met with success in my field.

When I was five years old, I met a woman then in her forties who was a successful landscape architect. She became my mentor. She introduced me to the possibility of this work as a profession. She inspired me with her great love of the outdoors, plants, and gardens. She showed me how landscaping enhances buildings. I can truly say she is responsible for my chosen profession. Throughout the years, she encouraged me and followed my career. I always felt very lucky to have someone I could talk to about our chosen field.

About five years ago, I landscaped a summer home completely on my own. Recently the owner of the home, in anticipation of a major political fund-raising event there, wanted to jazz up the landscaping. With a budget in mind, she approached several landscape architects and was turned down by all of them because they didn't feel the budget would produce the desired results. My mentor, however, took on the project.

What hurt was that she never talked to me about it. That felt like a slap in the face. I called her, but she never returned my call. I still don't understand why she didn't tell me herself that she had been approached for this project and was planning on doing it. Had she simply checked in with me and we had talked about how each of us felt, I would have been fine. Instead, I feel betrayed by her. I know she must feel guilty. There's no other excuse for her silence.

She recently had an eighty-fifth birthday party, and I wasn't even invited. This is a woman I have known almost my whole life, a woman who is nearing the end of hers, a woman who nurtured me as I established myself in our profession. It's very upsetting to me still, and I hate to think of her dying without our clearing the air between us.

I've always looked forward to being a mentor myself. This experience has taught me how important trust is between friends, be they mentors or peers.

—SAMANTHA, 45, NEW YORK CITY

Comment:
If the friend acknowledges her behavior and apologizes, the friendship can continue. It's never too late to forgive a friend when she is accountable.

Diane's Diary

After my father died, I started keeping a journal again. It had been years and years since I had done so. When I was about thirteen, my grandmother gave me a little diary with a lock and key. I had just won an essay contest at school, and this was her way of encouraging me in my writing. I loved writing in it and putting down all my hopes and dreams. One day, however, my mother let something slip. It was something that was only in my diary. I discovered there was a second key and that my mother had been reading my diary all along. That day, I stopped writing and hadn't felt the impulse again until my father died.

I bought myself a pretty notebook with quotes about women at the bottom of each page. I recorded my thoughts about my father and how much I missed him. It was sort of like carrying on a conversation with him. I was very honest and truthful. It felt good to be writing again, as I had always loved to write.

An old friend from my hometown came for a visit and stayed for almost a week. Some weeks after the visit, we were talking, and she mentioned something about my uncle. It was something that was not widely known, but I had written about it in my journal, which I had kept on my bedside table. I was so stunned that I asked her point-blank if she had read my journal while she was visiting. She admitted she had, excusing her actions by saying, "Well, it was there." Sure, beneath a stack of magazines, under a lamp!

I felt totally betrayed by her, and, in fact, the incident has ended our friendship completely. Once again, I stopped writing. I just didn't feel safe anymore putting down my private thoughts.

However, on a recent flight (I'm a flight attendant), I spotted a pretty journal on a passenger's table, and I paused to ask her about it. We ended up talking on and off for about an hour. I told her both of my betrayal stories, and still she encouraged me to take up writing again. She recommended a particular book for me to read that advocates journalizing, and she told me how much her own journalizing had meant to her. So I'm going to put my past experiences aside, find a new pretty book, and give it another try. This time, however, I think I'll find a better hiding place, at least to start.

—DIANE, 40, SAN JOSE, CA

Loyalty Pays

When I met my husband, he was dating my best friend. Though I learned subsequently that he was interested in me right away, I didn't give him a single thought because he was my best friend's beau. For me, friends' beaus were off-limits.

Jeff, however, swung into action. First, he broke up with my friend. Then he went to great lengths to fix her up. Not until the third try, when she liked the guy, did Jeff ask me out. In the meantime, he simply made up excuses to keep in touch with me. He said later he didn't want me to forget him.

Finally, with my friend settled into a new relationship, he made his move. He knew I was thinking of changing jobs, so he asked me out to dinner to talk about venture capital, which is what he does. I thought we were going to have a nice, professional dinner, but instead he took me to an engagement party where I knew no one and everyone, it seemed, had heard of me already. Finally, I got the idea he was very interested in me.

However, before I continued going out with him, I had lunch with my friend and told her Jeff had asked me out. I asked her if she minded if I went out with him and told her I wouldn't go out with him if it bothered her. She said she didn't mind. With that, Jeff and I began dating and three years later were married.

A couple of years after Jeff and I started dating, my friend and I were talking over drinks. She revealed that she had, in fact, been very upset when I told her Jeff had asked me out. However, she realized she and Jeff didn't have a future even though she liked him, and she hadn't wanted to stand in the way. But she was very appreciative of my being straightforward with her and of my putting our friendship first.

I believe I did the right thing checking with her before I started dating Jeff. Her friendship meant much more to me at that point than my relationship with Jeff. In hindsight, my friend did me a favor by not speaking her mind. The trust she felt in me because of my honesty and the respect I showed our friendship has made our friendship that much richer. She is still my dear friend, and we trust each other even more now.

—TRACEY, 35, ATHERTON, CA

Comment:

Incidents between friends where loyalty is paramount cement the friendship.

SIX

~

Courage in
Friendships

*C*ourage is about being as conscious as possible so that we know who we are and what our stand is. Courage is about living our lives true to our own beliefs and convictions, listening to our own inner voice first and not letting others persuade us to do something we know in our hearts we don't want to do or isn't right to do. It is also about sticking to our beliefs or knowing when it is right to step away.

Courage starts with how we live our own lives. Then it radiates out to those around us, be they family, friends, or even strangers. Being courageous in our friendships is about doing the right thing with regard to a friend. This may mean standing by her or being her witness and taking a stand for her regardless of outside pressures. It may also take courage to present our truth to her if we feel she needs to hear that, even if we know we have different opinions. Disagreements and difficulties are inevitable.

Yvonne and Andi, competitive tennis partners, lost a doubles match they should have won easily. Andi knew she was off her game, had been for some time, and felt responsible for the loss. Overcoming her fear that right after a humiliating loss was not the best time for such a discussion, Yvonne, instead of blaming Andi, gently suggested that Andi was showing signs of being menopausal. She herself had just gone through it and recognized the signs. At first, Andi didn't think it was possible, but she consulted a doctor, who confirmed what Yvonne had said. Andi thanked her friend for taking a risk and speaking up. With Andi on Hormone Replacement Therapy, they trounced their next opponents.

It is when we have problems that our courage is tested. And it is how we are at these times that affects a friendship: either we move to a new, deeper level of intimacy because we have the courage to address the problem, or we pull away because we don't.

Blair and Lisa, old friends who hadn't seen each other for a while, spent a weekend together. Every time Blair shared an opinion with Lisa, Lisa took the opposite point of view. Whenever Blair made an observation, however small, amusing or serious, Lisa failed to react. They parted with Blair feeling lonely and disconnected. She wished she'd had the courage to speak up and tell her friend how she was feeling. Had she done that perhaps she would have felt understood and accepted by the friend.

Most of us expect a friend to be there for us. Sometimes a friend is stopped by her fears, afraid to speak up or take a stand that might be unpopular in the outside world. When this happens, we come to a crossroads in the friendship. We may decide to accept her inability to be brave on our behalf and continue the friendship despite our disappointment and hurt, or we may decide that courage in a friend is too important to ignore.

If we were never stopped by fear, we would be true to ourselves at all times, live no-limit lives, and be a very good friend. Courage is about acknowledging our fears and deciding to go for it anyway because we know we are doing the right thing. We want our closest friends to feel the same way.

Caring Enough to Be Tough

For one week each autumn, six friends and I meet in the Caribbean, aboard a fifty-one-foot sailboat, and sail the British Virgin Islands. We grew up in the same town in the South, and I don't remember a time when I didn't know these women. Some of us still live there, others don't. Some of us have been close friends since childhood, others hadn't seen each other for many years prior to the first sail.

This may sound like a story about sailing, but it's really a story about salvation and the healing power of friends. Because the one who started all this needed saving. Jill, whose father owns the boat and who planned the first sailing trip, drank heavily. No matter how big a boat is, it's still very close quarters. There are no secrets. Jill's drinking was not only obvious, it was an obvious problem. As the week progressed and Jill's unhappiness and behavior permeated the boat, the rest of us knew we could no longer stand by and watch our friend self-destruct.

Three months and many phone calls later, we joined her family and did an intervention. She voluntarily agreed to go for treatment. It took courage for us to confront her, but there is both safety and power in numbers. Jill simply couldn't deny her problem when the six of us had watched her practically through a microscope on that sail. Jill also couldn't deny that our action was coming from the love we have had for her for years.

In hindsight, it almost seems she'd instigated the whole trip as a cry for help. With our continued support and involvement in her recovery, Jill has stayed dry since. Knowing we risked losing a lifelong friend, we showed courage by going out on a big limb anyway in the hopes of saving her life. She, in turn, showed greater courage by going through the difficult process of getting dry. But she wasn't alone. We all eagerly anticipate our next reunion, made all the more special because we have our friend back.

—KATHERINE, 43, ATLANTA

Comment:

It takes courage to confront a friend who is engaged in self-destructive behavior because we are putting ourselves on the line and risking both the friend's wrath and the loss of the friendship. When we don't speak up, we stay stuck in a small, fearful frame of mind that does neither ourselves nor our friend any good. To be courageous ennobles us because we are being true to ourselves, our values, and our love for our friend.

Facing Death Together

I have a close friend whose husband died last year. During his illness their many friends, of which I am one, surrounded them, supporting her and John. But when it became clear that he was really dying, nobody knew how to acknowledge this next step, least of all my friend, Joan. We just weren't very skilled in how to deal with the stark reality of death.

We all tiptoed around Joan and John, keeping up a cheerful front and never alluding to anything that touched upon his leaving this earth. I could see that they were doing the same dance with each other, neither one able to speak of his or her deepest fears and pains. They were both shutting the other one out. I remember clearly one day when I was alone with Joan. I don't know where my words came from, but I suddenly asked her how she was feeling, knowing that any day John would die and that they hadn't ever even talked about this with each other.

Joan broke down and said that she'd been in tremendous pain (and she knew John was, too) not knowing how to address John's situation with him. She said that she yearned to, but every time she began, he would turn away; she just couldn't get past all his defensive barriers. Neither one was particularly religious, and she had no idea what to do. I suggested she talk to a friend of mine, a minister, which she did; upon her return she went to her husband, sat by his side, and began to tell him in very simple words that she knew he was dying and how she felt about it.

When she began to open up her heart and articulate her sadness to John, he responded in kind. He told her that he knew his time to go was soon, but that he hadn't been able to bring himself to face this. He said he was so afraid and also so sad. They held hands and talked and cried. He told her many things he'd never dared to before. By Joan's acknowledging his impending death, she gave herself and him permission to say good-bye and to go to that much deeper level of connection.

She told me later that during the last week of John's life, she had never seen him happier. Their accepting his death rather than denying it allowed John to complete what he needed to do before he died and also enabled them to truly embrace all that was important to them. She thanked me for being the friend who made her face what was happening. She told me that it's been the greatest gift any friend has ever given her.

—SARA, 42, MINNEAPOLIS, MN

Comment:
Even in the most emotionally painful situations, it is important to be courageous and get to the heart of the matter and speak up.

When Brave Is Best

I have known the woman I call my best friend for twenty-five years. I have lots of good stories about our friendship, but this one is about how we almost stopped being friends.

We have been close for all but one of those years. It was around the time my father died. I wasn't particularly close to him. She knew he was a mystery to me, since we had discussed our families at length. However, his sudden death really threw me. In hindsight, I now believe I went into deep mourning more for the father I never had than for my actual father. Back then, I didn't understand why I was so sad. To me, my friend seemed rather unsympathetic. I felt she assumed, based on what I had told her, that I shouldn't be that upset. I thought that since my friend hadn't lost a parent she couldn't understand what it felt like, regardless of what the parent-child relationship had been.

I got very hurt, unable to talk to her about why his death hit me so hard and why my feelings were so hurt. My way of expressing my hurt was to shut her out. I simply stopped seeing her. Around a year later, she called me out of the blue and asked if we could give our friendship another chance. She said she had missed me, and I knew I had missed her. We got together and talked about what had happened between us. I had started therapy during that year and had begun to understand my relationship with my father. But she was the brave one, and I have always been very grateful to her that she took the chance to make the overture to me and rekindle our friendship.

Since then, we have taken bigger and bigger emotional risks with each other. Her own father died recently after a long illness, and that brought us closer still. We don't always see eye to eye, but I value her honesty highly, as well as her bravery. She wasn't afraid to face rejection then, and we both learned a lot about pushing the envelope of our friendship.

—MK

Fight or Flight

Following college, I spent some time living in Puerto Rico with my parents and working. A friend from the States taught school there, and she often spent weekends at our house. Late one stormy afternoon, we took a walk on the neighborhood beach. The rain had finally stopped. Only a warm, wet wind and swiftly moving dark clouds remained of the storm. The beach was deserted except for debris like broken palm fronds, felled coconuts, storm-tossed seaweed, and an assortment of broken shells.

Dressed in very short skirts, as the fashion then dictated, we walked along chatting loudly to be heard over the wind. Suddenly, I felt something up under my dress. It was a hand giving me a very firm pinch. A scream from my friend told me she felt the same thing. We both whipped around to see a small man lunge toward us again. My friend immediately ran away, but something—anger, perhaps, or righteous indignation—made me challenge this interloper.

As he came toward me, our eyes locked. I planted both bare feet firmly in the wet sand and pushed him away with both hands against his small chest. He looked surprised, fell back slightly, but then recovered and pushed back against my shoulders. His push was hard enough to cause me to lose my balance. We were at the surf's edge, and I fell on my back into the warm, shallow water. He started to climb on top of me. I bent both legs, aimed them directly at his groin, and hit my mark with as much force as I could muster. I saw the shock and pain on his face as he reacted to the blow. I struck hard enough for him to fall off of me and into the surf. He quickly scrambled to his feet and ran off down the beach.

Adrenaline pumping through me, I stood up, smoothed my soaking wet hair and clothes, and ran over to my friend, who had watched my confrontation from some safe distance away. I remember, at the time, she seemed more upset than I was. We slowly walked back to my house, talking about what had happened. My whole body was shivering, but I felt strangely exhilarated. Perhaps I was even in mild shock.

My mind raced as well. In those few minutes, my feelings toward her changed. The closer to my house we got, the angrier I felt at her behavior. She talked as if something—other than that initial pinch—had happened to her. She said nothing about what I had been through, only how scared she had been. She seemed totally oblivious to the fact that she had run away, abandoning me. I couldn't believe how she had acted.

That was my first direct experience with the fight or flight mechanism. I don't believe we can predict how we will react in a dangerous situation. We can speculate that we would stay and fight because most of us would like to think we would be courageous, but theory and practice are two different things. Strangely, as I recollect the event, I don't believe I ever felt I had been in any real danger. I simply acted. And yet I reacted so quickly that I didn't take time to assess my opponent other than in a very cursory manner. What if he had been larger? What if he had had a knife or a gun? What if he had been determined to rape me rather than just be a pest, as I believe was the case?

This incident happened years ago when we were both very young. We never discussed our feelings about what happened that day. At that time I wasn't capable of expressing anger effectively. I didn't tell her how angry I was that she had run away. I didn't tell her that I thought she had been a chicken. I kept all those feelings bottled up.

Nor did she tell me how she felt. Maybe she had been really scared. Maybe she thought she was doing the prudent thing and that I was a total fool to try and fight the guy. Maybe she was ashamed of her behavior. We never gave each other the chance to see the incident from the other's perspective. We never gave ourselves the chance to clear the air. As a result, for me, the friendship ended that day. Circumstances were such that it was easy for us to fall out of touch, but I certainly never went out of my way.

We have many opportunities to make choices about who we stay friends with, how intimate we become with them, how committed we are to them, and so on. Most of us have a whole range of friends, from true intimates to what my mother calls "casual acquaintances." The reasons vary greatly how or when and why we move from one level of friendship to another deeper one or pull back and close ourselves off to someone. But in this case, and at this time in our young lives, I learned enough about her not to feel I could count on her. I learned I was a fighter and she wasn't. I also learned I wanted my friends to be fighters, too. The bottom line is that I would never have left her to fend for herself. She let me down and that destined her to become a former friend. Add to my attitude the fact that we never talked things through and there was no possible alternative.

Over the years, I rarely thought about that day and seldom spoke about it. When I did, I thought more of her abandonment and my unexpressed anger toward her than about the attack itself. Back then, I had almost no experience dealing effectively with anger and disagreement and being able to express negative emotions constructively to someone else. I also didn't know the cost of not bringing up difficult issues, of not talking through differences. When we can't and don't, we are destined to remain stuck in our negative feelings. There is no real room for growth and change, for resolution and forgiveness.

I don't know whether this woman and I would have stayed friends. Geographical separation alone might have been enough to bring the relationship to a close, but I do know we never could have become the kind of intimate friends I now treasure because we were not able to go through that incident in sufficient detail truly to understand each other's perspective.

—MK

My Friend Ellie

Ellie Sharp, who just celebrated her ninety-second birthday—almost forty years older than I—is one of my closest friends. When she turned eighty, I wrote a piece on her for the *Nob Hill Gazette* entitled "Active at Eighty." I talked of her love of life, her athletic prowess, and her proficiency in skiing, tennis, golf, and shooting. I mentioned that she had been written up in a national magazine as the first woman "to break the barrier," that is, the first woman ever to be accepted into a duck club, traditionally an all-male domain. What I didn't say was how much I loved her and how she was for me the mother I'd lost when I was twenty-two.

The year Ellie was eighty-five, we were both up at Sugar Bowl, a well-known ski resort in the Sierras, and Ellie had been asked to forerun the Silver Belt Giant Slalom Masters Race, a very challenging course that wound its way down a double black diamond run. It had snowed all night; a winter storm watch was in full alert. That morning she was up early, stretching and getting ready for the race. By the time she got onto the chairlift, alone of course, the winds were blowing gale force, visibility was almost zero, and most of the other chairlifts had been shut down.

While Ellie waited in freezing conditions for over an hour on top of the mountain, race officials deliberated about whether or not to cancel the race. The storm abated somewhat, and they decided to go ahead. Waiting anxiously near the bottom, I finally saw her coming, a tiny dot skiing down the Steilhung, a steep face ringed by rocky cliffs that dropped perpendicularly down to the flats.

Two minutes and fifty seconds later, Ellie crossed the finish line. When I went over to give her a hug, she said, "Snow is great, but God, it's cold. I'm going into the bar and get a hot toddy." And then she was off, a wisp, all five feet and ninety-eight pounds, in a bright red powder ski suit disappearing into the falling snow. I didn't get the chance to say how gutsy I thought she was.

I just stood there, relieved that she was safe, in awe of her courage and physical stamina. I don't know of any other eighty-five-year-old who would have—or could have—skied in a Sierra storm such as that one, much less run one of the most difficult race courses around. But Ellie just never lets her age interfere with whatever it is she decides to do; it is simply not an issue for her.

For the rest of us, it is. Most of us stop taking such risks. We grow older timidly; instead of big steps, we start to tiptoe through our life. The scope of our world shrinks. We begin hanging onto railings to keep ourselves from falling, we avoid double black diamond ski runs and ski the pack instead, we rent golf carts to carry our bags, and we think twice before meeting new people or venturing into uncharted waters. We say no instead of yes. Not Ellie.

This past summer my husband and I, together with some other friends, invited Ellie to go with us on a five-day fishing trip on the remote Smith River in Montana. Without a moment's hesitation, she accepted, thrilled to be able to experience this adventure. "Oh, how Jim [her husband, who died twenty years ago] would have loved this," she said more than once, as she was floating down the Smith, bamboo rod in one hand and binoculars in the other, as she watched an eagle circle overhead.

I remember one clear, black, starry night when we were all sleeping outside. The full moon was coming up late behind the dark cliffs, outlining them in threads of silver, and we heard some coyotes howl off in the distance. Ellie, tucked tight into her down bag, turned to me saying, "If this isn't Heaven, I don't know what is." For me it was, too.

Over the years, Ellie, a member of one of the best duck clubs in California, has frequently invited my husband and me to go duck hunting with her. This winter, right before her ninety-second birthday, we were once again her guests.

As I stumbled along in the dark, my waders awkward and bulky, my gun making a painful dent in my shoulder, I looked ahead at Ellie, who was, of course, leading the way. We came to the edge of a deep pond, and I could barely discern the outlines of our destination, the duck blind, some two hundred yards off in the middle of Adams Lake. Ski pole in one hand and her gun over her shoulder, Ellie, without hesitation, climbed down the bank and began wading out to the blind. The farther she went, the deeper the water became, and I watched worriedly as it came right up to the top of her waders.

I was next. Gingerly, I stepped into the water and then stopped dead in my tracks. Memories of an old duck club and walking out to a blind surrounded by potholes into which I invariably would fall came flooding back to me. I couldn't make my feet move in the slippery mud. Then I looked up and saw her, alone out there in the lake with her dog, Coot, swimming nearby. Her head was tilted upward toward the sky. Some ducks were flying over, faintly outlined by the first light of dawn creeping over the eastern foothills. She motioned to me to hurry up; it was time to shoot. I began that long walk toward her.

I can't pinpoint Ellie's secret. She says it's because she exercises every day, whether it's playing tennis or golf and lugging her own clubs around the course, or whether she's shooting, fishing, or skiing. She speculates that because she's danced, ballet and ballroom, all her life, she's kept her muscles in shape. I'm sure she's right; keeping active physically is one key to leading a long and full life. But there's much more involved in her success. She is a woman who loves life, embraces it, and shares it wholeheartedly with her friends.

For me, she is an ongoing inspiration; she shows me the way. Whenever I'm despairing, I only have to conjure up an image I have of Ellie in Montana last summer. It's late in the afternoon before cocktail hour has started, and she is on her way down to the river. She is wearing a vibrant pink bathing suit. She tells me she wants to float on her back and watch the swallows swoop down and skim across the water. Besides, she adds, it's that time of day when you can see the mountains most clearly reflected in the smooth eddies of the river.

—LB

Comment:

When a friend leads her life with courage, she sets an example for the rest of us to follow. Her acts of courage not only make us more aware of how we limit ourselves but also inspire us to open up to as many opportunities in life as we possibly can. A courageous friend continually lights our way.

Taken by Surprise

When I married, I moved to where my husband was working. I had to leave all my old friends and start over. Soon after I settled in, I met a woman my age who was my next-door neighbor.

We became best friends, had babies together, and worked side by side in our community. We were also passionately involved in women's issues, and so our friendship spanned many areas of common ground: housewife, mother, neighbor, community activist.

One day she was next door, and the next day she was gone. She simply left—husband, children, everything. She discarded her whole previous life. She called me and told me that she was a lesbian and had moved in with another woman. You'd think we might have talked about all this, but we never did, and so I was taken by surprise at this drastic change in her life. Even though I was stunned and hurt that she hadn't felt she could confide in me, I was prepared to support her and remain her friend, no matter what choices she made.

But I didn't get the chance to support her. The woman Mary moved in with just did not want her to see me anymore. She simply would not condone it. Mary went along with her and allowed her to dictate who she could see and who she couldn't. Without a word, Mary just let our friendship go as if it had never had any meaning for her.

On top of Mary's keeping her secret from me, I was equally hurt that she didn't have the courage to stay my friend. The emotional aftermath of her decision stayed with me a long time. Seven years later when she wrote me a letter of apology, it was too late. I wish her well, but I need a friend who is loyal and courageous enough to take a stand as I was willing to do for her.

—PAMELA, 54, BERKELEY, CA

Comment:

Courage starts with being ourselves, acknowledging our entire nature. In courageous friendship, we share our whole self. Our friend does as well, and we accept each other. In courageous friendship we stand by our friend.

Don't Rock the Boat

Karen and I were college roommates and have been friends for over thirty years. Recently, Marj, a new friend to both of us, acted in a very mean-spirited way toward me. When I tried to talk to Marj about my hurt feelings, she refused to acknowledge that she'd done anything wrong.

Subsequently, every time I saw Marj—which was frequently, since our daughters were friends and schoolmates—she would make a big point of not answering when I said hello. She would even move should I happen to sit next to her.

I told Karen what had happened and how unhappy I was, fully expecting (because of our long-term friendship) that she would sympathize and perhaps even say something to Marj like "I'm sad that you hurt my friend Lee; I don't like how you've treated her." But Karen said nothing and did nothing to address the problem. Instead she simply continued her friendship with Marj.

In choosing the safe, cowardly way of pretending not to know that I was hurt in any way, Karen was giving Marj the message that "It's O.K. with me that you've hurt my friend; I'm not going to rock the boat." Karen wanted to be friends with both of us, but in reality her not challenging Marj was more important to her than standing up for me and our friendship.

How I wish Karen had had the courage to speak up for me and to be loyal to our friendship. Maybe if she had, Marj might have learned something valuable about how to treat friends.

This experience has made me more aware of the complications of friendship and has also distanced me from my college friend. I no longer trust her as much as I did before; now there are subjects I don't feel safe bringing up with her. It is easy to be a good friend when the stakes aren't high. But when they are, that's what separates the close friend from the fair-weather friend who won't take sides because she might lose out on something.

It would never occur to me not to stand up to someone who had acted in a damaging way to a friend of mine, so it was particularly disappointing when someone I had regarded as a close friend didn't do this for me. If Karen had been courageous and spoken to Marj about what happened, and Marj had been accountable, we all could have moved on in friendship together.

—LEE, 39, ANN ARBOR, MI

Comment:
We can always forgive a friend when she is accountable. Both accountability and forgiveness take courage.

The Courage to Stay a Friend

I have a friend of many years who went through a bitter divorce a few years back. During custody hearings, my friend asked me to be a character witness for her. Since I had known her and her husband well and had been a guest in their home many times, it was a difficult situation to have to take sides so completely. But evidence had piled up that led me to be convinced that my loyalties lay with my friend, the wife. Nonetheless, on the day of the hearing, my heart was pounding as the husband and his lawyer passed by and I saw the anger on his face as he looked at me.

Although theirs had been a rocky relationship for years, he clung fiercely to the marriage. When my friend wanted out, he turned on her and did what he could to hurt her, including incurring huge legal bills. The details are less important than how I have felt about my behavior.

I am probably proudest of my friendship with her because it tested me. It tested my integrity and loyalty and forced me to examine what had happened and come up with my own opinion of the truth. I stood by her. I went to court with her. I confronted the husband in writing, on the phone, and face to face. I do not consider myself to be a brave person, but I was brave for her. And I learned it wasn't even that hard because I loved her and believed her ex-husband had behaved inappropriately. In my opinion, he refused to be accountable for the pain he inflicted on others, especially my friend.

Because of my friendship with her, I am now clear that there are people in my life for whom I will take a stand. I haven't had to put that to the test much. But I did for her. She helped me see I don't have to be ruled by fear of some elusive authority figure, that I am capable of determining what is the truth for me. Her needing me to be brave for her was as great a gift to me as my being there was to her.

—MK

Comment:
Sometimes we have to speak up and take a stand for a friend with no thought of how it will impact us in the outside world. We do this because we know it is the right thing to do.

SEVEN

~

Being Conscious in Friendships: Final Reflections

*T*hose of us who embrace the spiritual in our lives may or may not align ourselves with a formal religion and may or may not talk about a "religious" life. But whether we call ourselves a Christian, Jew, Hindu, Buddhist, Muslim, or none of the above, we accept that there are basic laws of the universe: those of God and goodness. We try to live by these laws, acknowledging that there is a greater good, which requires us to take responsibility for how we live our lives. What we share in common is the way we want to relate to ourselves, to others, and to the world at large.

How we live our life day to day is the true measure of our spiritual and emotional awareness. Do we show a basic respect for others regardless of their age, sex, race, or the kind of job they have? Or do we make judgmental comparisons that find the other person lacking in some way? Do we listen to and acknowledge other points of view, or do we always have to be right? Do we treat ourselves and others with love and kindness, or are we impatient or mean?

Being conscious involves a willingness to face the truth about ourselves and be able to change. It is a commitment to inner growth, to the development of emotional awareness, and to enlarging the sense of our own responsibility. Deepening awareness evolves out of the choices we make, whether we act willfully and succumb to our own gratification or whether we acknowledge a higher principle, follow our conscience, and do what we know is right.

Life is filled with choices. Selfish ones do nothing to further our consciousness. Conversely, the more choices we make in favor of goodness and love, the more we embrace our spiritual nature. In other words, consciousness and responsibility equate with spiritual growth.

Conscious friendship is friendship between people who follow a path toward wholeness. We see ourselves and our friends as part of a larger whole. We want to make the right choices for ourselves and for our friends, and we expect our friends to do the same. If we happen not to, we acknowledge that we didn't and strive to do better the next time. We want our friends to support our efforts and forgive us, just as we would them.

The Bridge of Angels

For me friendship is a deep commitment to showing my true self to another person. It takes courage to reach out to a friend and lay bare my soul. With friendship I visualize a set of building blocks that I lay one on top of another; these are blocks of trusting, risking, trusting again, then allowing myself the risk of being vulnerable one more time. I think the strongest friendships have evolved in this way.

When they embrace a belief in a higher power, then the best of friends can go to deep levels of spirituality. I like to feel that I am building a stairway up to the angels, so that no matter how many storms and broken bridges I might encounter, I am still with the angels.

I have a picture from my childhood that I keep visible above my desk. Two children are holding hands and are about to step out onto a bridge on a wild, stormy night. The bridge crosses over a deep river gorge, and in the middle it's broken and swaying back and forth in the wind. But there is an angel there guiding them, and they believe in her. Without the angel, the power of the storm might engulf the children or one might push the other one off to save herself. We absolutely need that spiritual awareness in our friendships.

—MERCEDES, 54, PALO ALTO, CA

A Montana Storm

I've been wondering if it's possible to be close friends with another person without sharing some sort of spiritual connection. By this I don't mean that we have to sit around pondering God or that we attend church together or even join a Bible study group. It's more a shared, unspoken understanding in a power greater than ourselves.

Some of my most spiritual friends rarely talk about their beliefs, but their spirituality shines through in the way they live their lives and relate to the people around them. It's how a friend treats her child or how she listens clearly and gently to another person; it's an innate acknowledgment of kindness and consideration of themselves and others.

I am always attracted to people like this. My closest friends do share with me a belief in God and His laws of goodness, and even though at times we are unsuccessful in following this path, we know we have each other to turn to for understanding. I feel lucky to be able to share this part of myself with a friend.

I remember clearly one day early last summer when my best friend, Maria, and I were hiking. We came upon a beautiful field of wildflowers. Without saying anything we both lay down, head to head. Far off in the west, we could see thunderheads building up and hear faint rumblings, which we knew were heralding the approach of a typical Montana storm. I impulsively asked her how she imagined God, and she told me that she felt Him everywhere and especially right then when we were alone, flat on our backs, and looking upward to that dark blue sky.

I will never forget that feeling of deep connection we had, which has become the defining force in our friendship.

—KAY, 52, HELENA, MT

Comment:
There are times when we are alone with a friend in the majesty of nature and our mutual love and respect for its strength and beauty bring us together in a deeply connected way.

A Friend's Shining Example

I have a friend, Sandy, whom I have known since I was seventeen, who inspires me all the time because of her positive attitude toward life despite great hardship. At twenty-seven, after two miscarriages, she was diagnosed with ovarian cancer. We were very close at that time, and never once did she express any thoughts about dying. She was extremely positive during the whole process, including the awful treatment. Her focus was always on the future and being healthy again. Despite the seriousness of her prognosis, not only did she survive, she went on to have two children against overwhelming odds. Within seven years, she went through two additional traumas: the death of her mother, to whom she was very close, and the failure of her marriage. Her husband left her with her children to raise. Regardless, she has chosen to take all these difficult experiences and look at them as lessons for growth. Instead of becoming bitter and feeling victimized by all that has happened, she uses them to keep her heart open. This enables her to continue to look at the positive side of everything. What a difference her shining example has made for me. Whenever I'm feeling down, I think of Sandy and what she's been through. That helps me see what I can learn from the hard times, putting in perspective anything I'm going through. By her example, she helps me see that I have a choice about how I'm going to deal with the inevitable challenges of life.

—NANCY, 35, SONOMA, CA

Comment:

When we have a friend who continually says "Yes!" to life, who accepts and understands life's pains and obstacles, realizing that great good comes from them, that friend serves as a shining example to us all.

Emotional Intelligence

We hear so much about abstract intelligence, concrete intelligence, IQs, and SATs. We push our children to achieve academically, knowing that the world judges success on straight A's and the highest test scores. Until recently, little attention was paid to the world of feelings and intuition. With the recent success of Daniel Goleman's book *Emotional Intelligence*, now suddenly there's all this talk about the importance of emotional intelligence, about how it should be considered seriously as a yardstick of how successful a child will be later in life.

I couldn't agree more. Some of the smartest people I know are amazingly emotionally undeveloped; they have great skills in using a computer, analyzing the stock market, or litigating, but little ability to relate to people around them in a real and empathetic way. There's a whole part of their life that's atrophied, and while they might be earning lots of money and serving on many boards, they feel unfulfilled and frustrated with their lives.

Emotional intelligence begins with self-awareness. When we practice listening to our own thoughts and feelings with kindness, when we recognize ourselves, then we can create a relationship of empathy that extends to others around us. Emotionally intelligent people are sensitive to others' feelings; they respect another's perspective and are able to listen, without defensiveness, to opinions and ideas different from their own.

They are willing to share themselves with others, thus building a community of dialogue and an authentic emotional interchange. These habits of the heart are integral to the authenticity of any relationship, including friendship. The more developed our emotional intelligence becomes, the deeper and more rewarding our friendships and everything else in our life will be.

Conversely, the less emotionally intelligent we are, the more we are willing to perpetuate unhealthy friendship. We are then susceptible to the dark side of friendship, the shadowed side where vulnerability, trust, consciousness, truthfulness, accountability, empathy, and authenticity rarely surface.

—LB

Comment:

Fortunately we are realizing more and more that there are different kinds of intelligence and different ways of learning and demonstrating our talents—all valid and valuable. Perhaps that friend who is emotionally intelligent—self-aware and empathetic—is the friend that those who are really "smart" will value.

Simple Grace

Journal entry, written on the day my mother died:

For days I have focused on my mother's body, on her sallow skin, her dry mouth, her shiny forehead, her mottled hands bruised from the IVs. In all the countless acts of caring I have forgotten that I have a body, too.

Around dusk, my best friend, Sally, offers me a back rub. She works on the indentations in my neck, on my shoulders, and my forearms, releasing the muscles that are hanging on to last details. If I let go of mother's life, what will take its place? Who will touch me with her simple grace?

What's so often missing from friendship today is the life of the body. More and more we are separated from our blood ties. We do not live with the bodies that bore us but in the midst of strangers whom we have not yet made into "familiars." As we age, the freedom to touch is something that must be granted. Even earned.

Sally and I have known each other twenty years, yet we've never brushed each other's hair or huddled beneath the quilts as siblings do on rainy days. As an only child, I used to like the warmth of the litter, the sweaty comfort of tangled arms and legs. Perhaps, on occasion, that's what friends need from one another—a place to be held and "mothered," to feel known and safe.

This ease of contact belongs to childhood, to an age of careless innocence. For adults, so proud of their autonomy and independence, intimacy requires courage and, at times, a leap of faith.

Beside my mother's bed is the book that I've been reading on the challenges of friendship as we age. The author, Stuart Miller, writes: "Bold acts of consciousness, I believe, are the basis for an art of friendship. Gradually you give up shame and embarrassment while still retaining an essential vulnerability. After all such acts, pray for grace."

After the loving back rub my hands are no longer locked. I no longer hold anything in them, no lists, no thoughts, no preparations, no objects to be washed or placed. I have been held and gentled, though the hands that formed me are oddly silent and brittle as a twig. Thanks to Sally's act of grace, I fall into a deep sleep where my mother's spirit waits, deep and silent like a river. Because my friend is with me, I am not afraid.

THIS IS AN EXCERPT FROM *GETTING USED TO LETTING GO*, ESSAYS ON THE RELATIONSHIP OF CREATIVITY AND LOSS, BY VALERIE ANDREWS, 50, SONOMA, CA

Comment:
Sometimes the simple act of touching a friend grounds her, reassuring her as much as any spoken words of comfort could do.

Can I Have Both?

I was worried that when I got married, I would lose touch with my women friends. After all, I was now a couple, and couples are supposed to socialize together. But after a while I realized that there was room enough for both my husband and my girl-friends. They provided certain avenues for intimacy that my husband didn't, and I came to the conclusion that I was being unrealistic expecting him to meet all my needs.

My women friends offer me new perspectives and expose me to situations I might not experience with my husband. These friendships enrich my marriage rather than diminish it. I've found that it works well when a couple can see friends together and also have their own separate friends. Everyone wins.

—SARAH, 28, SALT LAKE CITY

> *Comment:*
> *Just because a woman gets married, her girlfriends need not lose their place. They can be important in a new way by giving her a perspective and an intimacy different from what her husband may offer.*

Befriend Ourselves First

Through my friendships I have learned some important lessons, the most important one being that we need first to be a friend to ourselves. This relationship is also the most difficult one to achieve. As women we're taught to take care of others, to disregard our own needs and feelings, and as a result we end up suffering, and this affects our friendships. I've come to realize that to be a good friend I must take care of myself first.

Many times it's been easier for me to be a friend to someone else than to myself. I am my own worst critic; I condemn myself too quickly. But I know that when I am kind to myself,

I am a better friend to others. Forgiveness and not judging someone else all go back to how I treat myself.

Too often I've wanted other people's approval, and so I've ended up compromising my own inner voice and hence not being a friend to myself. When I can be true and loyal to myself, I can then speak with my own voice and be a real friend to my friends.

—GEORGETTE, 50, NEW YORK CITY

Comment:
When we befriend ourselves and treat ourselves with loving kindness, we will be a good friend to others.

The Ditzy-Pat Star

I have a friend from childhood named Charlotte. Her mother, Ditzy, was my mother's best friend, and so, growing up, our lives were intertwined. When my mother died years ago, I turned to Ditzy as a surrogate mother. She simply stepped in where Mom had been and helped to fill that empty place.

When Charlotte was teaching in China last year, Ditzy died unexpectedly. I spent some time with my friend when she returned for the funeral, and she told me she had sent in to the U.C. Berkeley Astronomy Department to have a star named after both our mothers—the Ditzy-Pat Star.

Now I can see them every time I look up into a black, starry sky. I imagine them laughing and gossiping. They are both newlyweds again, eager and in love and ready to take on the world. They put their arms around each other's waist and walk in step, high heels clicking, purses swinging, gloves in hand, and certainly some wonderful scarf tucked around their necks. Just picturing them together, perhaps perched on this star, makes my pain subside.

Charlotte wrote me after she had returned to China. "It's cloudy and overcast in Chengdu, so I mostly stargaze in my mind. Still, in my imagination, I inquire, 'Star light, star bright, which star do I see tonight?' and the Ditzy-Pat Star always answers. I went to my Chinese church today, and Minister Li was telling the Christmas story. He ended it with a metaphor. The story is love. The power of association is a wondrous thing, and my mind became a mass of images of the beach. I was five years old and Ditzy and Pat were both watching over me through an oxygen tent. I remembered asthma, not being able to breathe, but I also remembered the touch of four maternal hands. Linda, we should be so proud of our mothers."

—LB

> ### Comment:
> Friendships cross all generations. When mothers are friends and their daughters follow suit, what a rich tapestry of emotions and memories we have.

Life Is Short

I tend to demand a lot from my friends. Life is short, and I think we forget that sometimes. I don't want chitchat. I don't want friends to keep me at a distance when I try to go to a deeper level.

I am reminded of some lines from the poem "The Art of Disappearing" by Naomi Shihab Nye:

Walk around feeling like a leaf.
Know you could tumble any second.
Then decide what to do with your time.

This poem makes me think twice about which friends I choose to spend my time with.

—MURIEL, 42, EUGENE, OR

Comment:
Live every day as if it could be your last and choose your friendships with that in mind.

Similar Wavelengths

For me close friendship is about similar emotional maturity. Where you are in your emotional and psychological development and what's going on inside you impacts the kind of friend you will choose to have. My friends now are very different from the ones I used to have.

For a long time in my life, I only wanted my friends to like me and not to disagree with me. We had an unspoken agreement that we would stroke each other and never say, "I don't like what you just did." I wasn't ready to look at myself other than in a superficial way, and that's what I expected from my friends.

Now I am committed to friends who are willing to change and who will challenge themselves and me. I also like women who are authentic, and by that I mean someone who is being real with me. She tells me how she's feeling, what she is doing, and what is going on inside of her. She does not put up a false front.

It takes courage to risk being real and vulnerable, and I've had to work on myself to become this way. Because I am changing and on a different emotional level now, some of my old friends are resisting this in me and in themselves. As a result I have lost them as close friends. But with this newfound ability to be more open and intimate, my new friendships are more rewarding.

—BETH, 51, SAN FRANCISCO

A Fish Story

Six years ago, my son, Nick, brought home two goldfish he'd won at the school fair. When he held out the plastic bag filled with water, I reached forward quickly to grab it, as it was leaking badly. Finding a small container I normally used for flowers, I unceremoniously dumped the contents in. One fish immediately rolled over and died, and Nick was desolate. I prepared him for the inevitable—that the other one wouldn't last much longer—but fortunately that didn't happen.

As eight-year-olds are prone to do, Nick soon lost interest in that lone fish he named Fred. I took over as the caretaker, and not a very solicitous one at that. Beyond the bare necessities of food and fresh water, I did nothing to make his home more interesting. Not an arch, plant, or rock brightened up his world.

Bizarre as it seemed to me, as time passed I became more attached to Fred. I'd worry when he didn't move around much; I thought he was dying, and I'd rap loudly on his six-inch bowl to get him moving. He'd perk up, darting quickly about, and I was relieved. The years went by, and he became a permanent fixture in our house. Mornings, I'd see him there and feel reassured. Evenings we'd gather around the kitchen table, and there would be Fred, circling around and around in his stark container.

Last summer, my husband and I went to Montana while Nick was at camp. We left our nineteen-year-old son, John, in charge of our house and Fred. Unknown to me he'd made the decision to set Fred free after we were well away on our vacation. He explained to me later that he could no longer bear to see him, day after day, confined to such a sterile environment. So he took him down to our tiny neighborhood church, which just happened to have a spring spilling out into a beautiful large pool of water in the center of the courtyard. One other fish, a larger one, was there alone.

When John put Fred in the water, he lay there, paralyzed, not knowing what to do, and tilted sideways, and John was worried that he would drown. But suddenly the larger fish came over and nudged Fred, righting him, and slowly they went off together, Fred swimming behind. John stayed for quite a while and watched as Fred got used to his new home. Never leaving each other's side, they swam everywhere, Fred imitating the actions of his new friend. When the older fish fed off the moss on the side, Fred did, too. When he swam underneath the fountain of water to hide, Fred went there as well, and when he streaked across the pond, Fred followed.

Returning from our vacation, I immediately went into the kitchen to check on Fred. He was nowhere to be found. Upset, I asked John what happened and he told me he had set Fred free. Disbelieving and worried about Fred's fate, I went down to see for myself. As I neared the pool, I saw the two fish together, feeding off the mossy walls. When they sensed my approach, they moved off under the small waterfall. Quietly, I sat down and watched them for a long time.

Many times I went to visit. One day recently I walked into the courtyard and saw a large metal pipe diverting the water from the spring. Going closer, I realized that all the water had been drained out, and Fred and his friend were gone. Right then I lost it; I started crying and crying. When I got home, I immediately called my close childhood friend, Mimi, and told her the entire story, starting from when Nick brought Fred home to his final disappearance.

I knew it was a bit strange that I'd gotten so attached to a fish, but I wasn't very clear on why Fred and all that had happened touched me so deeply. Listening closely, Mimi said she could well understand my feelings. Part of Fred's story, she explained, mirrored my own. Fred was strong; he was a survivor. He'd lasted for many years trapped in a small, suffocating cage, and then, when set free, not only adapted to his new surroundings but thrived and was happy. His death, coming so soon after his new life, was naturally upsetting.

Mimi's validation of my feelings comforted me, and her true understanding of my own experiences—resulting from our lifelong friendship—enabled me to have a clearer insight into myself. Another close friend, who is active in that very church and knew how upset I was, called the rector. Just a few days ago, she told me the good news—Fred and his friend are safe and will be returned to their wellspring as soon as the church construction is finished.

—LB

Comment:

At times friends help us to understand our own life more clearly. They have sufficient distance—and close-ness—to see something about our life that illuminates its meaning.

The Laboratory of Friendship

When I was much younger, I used to feel that if I disagreed with a friend, we couldn't be friends anymore. I guess I felt that dis-agreement meant we weren't really compatible, probably stem-ming from a feeling that love was conditionally based on some impossible standard of total compatibility.

What a relief that I am not burdened with that anymore! I just had tea with a dear friend where we successfully talked about a prior discussion we'd had when I hurt her feelings by expressing some opinions, which popped out of me rather indelicately because I had not yet realized that I was reacting to something she had proposed several days earlier that upset me. Convoluted? Yes, but not uncommon.

One of my life's goals is to close the gap between the time I hear something and the time I accurately identify how I feel about it. That way, I can react in the moment to my real feeling, rather than to my uneasiness, which may lead me to speak hastily from a defensive emotional position.

When I know how I'm feeling, I can speak from the heart. When I am not sure, I get into trouble. I get accusatory, overly negative, or defensive. And even as the words come out of my mouth, I know they are wrong. They are meant to defend and protect. They don't express the true underlying feeling because I don't know yet what that is.

A few days later my friend and I talked again when neither of us was feeling threatened or defensive. We really listened to each other and allowed ourselves to empathize with where the other was coming from.

At the end, we hugged and I said, "What a relief!" Our friendship could survive a disagreement, and I realized that part of the joy of friendship is working with the friend to maintain and deepen it, to process differences and to learn from each other.

—MK

Friendship Is a Gift

I have learned throughout my long life that true friendship is one of the greatest gifts we can receive. If you have just one real friend, then you can reach out and hold hands and walk through the difficult times with that person by your side. You can call that friend to share something wonderful that has happened to you, and you know that she will rejoice with you.

The sure way to have a friend is to be a friend. Never be afraid to tell your friend how much she or he means to you. True friends are to be cherished. I have been alone at times, but I have never felt truly lonely because I have been graced with Katherine as my friend.

—ESTHER, 85, PHOENIX, AZ

I'm So Cold

I had something incredible happen that helped me accept a world other than the concrete, visible one we live in day to day. I had never believed in anything I couldn't touch, see, or prove logically until the day after my mother died. That night, after locking up the entire house and turning on the alarm system, I went to bed, exhausted from the funeral. I fell asleep with the light on. Suddenly, I felt the pressure of someone sitting on my bed. I opened my eyes and saw my mother perched there by my side.

I was stunned, and before I could say a word, my mother, shivering and reaching out her arms to me, said, "Pat, I'm so cold, I'm freezing." Without thinking I hugged her and replied, "Mother, that's because you were always so cold to everyone in your life." Barely were the words out of my mouth than my mother disappeared. I sat there, silent and sad. I knew I'd been given an opportunity to feel closer to my mother, and I wished I hadn't said what I did.

Before this happened, I had never believed in life after death. However, this incident completely changed me. I began to reach out more and more to my family and friends. I can't explain it, but my heart just seemed to be wide open. As I became more loving, I was able to forgive my mother. And I embraced wholeheartedly my own spirituality, a dimension of life I had given little credibility to before my mother's bedside visit.

—PAT, 68, WASHINGTON, D.C.

How to Talk about God

I do not call myself Episcopalian, as I was baptized, Presbyterian as I grew up, or even exclusively a Christian. And yet, the faith in God I feel is strong and palpable, much more so than in my younger years when I might have identified myself with a particular religious affiliation.

But how do you talk to friends about God? I did not grow up talking to anyone about spiritual matters, other than to be preached to or taught. Belief was approached as an academic subject, not as the intense feeling it truly is. I didn't feel my faith because those who presented it to me weren't able to express how their own faith felt to them. Hence, religion became dry and fact-oriented. The sense of inexplicable wonder I felt at odd moments, moments in nature, for instance, or moments of feeling great love for someone, I now recognize as my innate belief in God, and I never lost that despite the dullness of my religious education. But I never talked to a friend about any of these special feelings.

Rather than use words, I believe I have to show my friends how my belief expresses itself in me and through me. I have to be open to feeling how a friend's belief expresses itself in her and through her. Faith is not about talking or explaining; it is about being.

—MK

Comment:

It is not what we say but who we are and how we live our lives that express our belief in God.

The Other Side of Power

I was raised in a family where great importance was placed on worldly power. Money, social position, the top job, and the biggest house were what counted. My father used these things to get what he wanted. I knew my mother disagreed with his value system, but she always went along with Dad's program. We had all the trappings of success. With their many connections they could open most any door they wanted, and this world of power and privilege filtered down to my siblings and me.

After my mother died, my father remarried, and with the arrival of my new stepmother, the entire power base in our family shifted. My older brother, long waiting to dethrone me, influenced my father and stepmother, and I could feel my power waning. Gradually, I became an outsider in my family.

Furthermore, the people in the social circles we frequented soon realized that if they continued to befriend me, they would risk my family's disapproval. They chose to drop me. These "friends" knew that there was no way I could offer anywhere near as much in terms of money, connections, and any sort of worldly power. And for them these things counted more than loyalty, authenticity, or real friendship. They stopped calling; they stopped inviting me to their parties. For them I wasn't important anymore. It was painful losing a place in my family and in the world I had grown up in, but even more painful watching as "friend" after "friend" left my side.

Before this time I had never given much thought to my friendships other than recognizing that I liked and enjoyed my friends and had fun running in the same circles with them. It wasn't until I lost my place that I faced the fact that friendships based on surface criteria such as money, social position, community visibility, or a CEO husband don't hold up very well. I began to realize that getting caught up in this world of superficial power ultimately prevents anyone from experiencing true intimacy and true friendship. It was also at this time that I began to revise my understanding of the meaning of power.

People who invest too much of themselves in this surface world aren't powerful at all. They have lost sight of what real power is, what writer Claude Steiner calls "the other side of power." He describes this as the power of love, intuition, communication, and creativity. I was fortunate enough also to have a few close friends who didn't buy into worldly power. They stayed by my side during this difficult time, and they helped me really see what is necessary for friendships to endure.

I have more true friends now than I had before, and I have learned an important lesson, one I will not forget. These friends, the ones who speak from their heart, are the people with real power. They understand what it means to be a friend.

—LB

> *Comment:*
> *What's important is not how many material possessions we have but how many true friends surround us. Look at the success of our life in terms of its emotional and spiritual richness, not in terms of how much money or wordly power we have. Love and loving relationships are where true power lies.*

Tell Me Who You're With and I'll Tell You Who You Are

I used to have friends who placed great importance on what they could get out of the friendship. I naively thought they liked me because of who I was inside, maybe because I had a good sense of humor or a creative flair. How wrong I was.

When it became obvious that being my friend wouldn't better their social position or their child's, when they realized I couldn't get them invited to the right parties, they dropped me. I remember one friend in particular who just stopped calling me when she discovered that I wasn't the one who could get her to the top of the heap.

At the time I was tremendously hurt. Now I see that these women base their friendships solely on who can do what for whom. I think our close friends are a reflection of who we are inside; chances are, if a woman's closest friend is interested only in superficial things, she will be as well.

There is a Spanish saying I found recently, which I've put on the wall of my study: "Tell me who you're with, and I'll tell you who you are." That, to me, says it all.

—SUSAN, 40, HARTFORD, CT

Comment:

In the eyes of a true friend, we will be able to see the grace and goodness of our own self, and if we share a deep, dark pain with her, we come away with a light shining from her eyes into ours. The friends we choose to surround ourselves with speak volumes about who we are as a person.

Afterword

*O*ne day a casual friend invited me for lunch to meet a woman who had just moved to San Francisco. I hesitated; my life was already full of commitments, leaving me little time to enjoy the friends I had. My husband and I were raising two young sons, I was involved in their school and other community projects, and I was also training on and off for national tennis tournaments.

But I accepted the invitation anyway and met Mary, who is now my co-author and my close friend. We hit it off immediately, finding we had many of the same interests—books, theater, a spiritual life, parenting, an appreciation of the outdoors, and a love of writing. We began sharing articles that touched us; we lent each other books. We read each other's writings and traded stories.

People and their stories have always fascinated me. Years ago I wrote many articles profiling interesting men and women. During this period I also met a woman new to town. We became fast friends and subsequently decided to write a book together about stepmothers. Unfortunately, we, as friends, parted ways before the project was finished and it was shelved.

Before this friendship failed, I took the fact that I had friends for granted. It wasn't until this friendship and several others ended that I really began to look at my friendships. Not only did I doubt my ability to be a good friend, I questioned why

I would stay in friendships that caused me pain. With the help of a therapist, I came to see myself more clearly, and this new-found consciousness helped me become a better friend, leading me to a deeper understanding of friendship.

I was eager to share my insights, and when I met Mary, I felt she might be just the friend with whom I could write about women's friendships. Because of the collapse of my previous writing collaboration, I was hesitant to approach her with my idea, but I finally decided to take a risk and ask if she were interested. She said yes, and our three-year journey of interviews and discussions of other women's stories about their friends began. In the process, we shared our own stories as well. I am forever grateful to all those women who told us their stories, and to my friend Mary, in particular.

Just as we learned from all the stories we heard, we also learned from each other. We began taking bigger risks, sharing more openly our feelings, opinions, discouragements, and triumphs. We weathered some disagreements as well. Our friendship grew over the course of writing this book, and we came to better understand what each of us needed and expected. As the book developed and gained form and content, so did our friendship.

I hope *Come Rain or Come Shine* will help all of us to be better friends, both to ourselves and to others. For sure, I am not the perfect friend; I have disappointed and hurt friends many times. But I see now that my failures, together with my successes, have contributed to make me the friend I am today.

—LB

The idea of writing a book on women and friendship was Linda's, as was the idea to write it with me. We were relatively new friends at the time, and I remember feeling very complimented.

It's hard to say how our friendship influenced the book or how the book influenced our friendship. Our friendship has benefited greatly from the stories we heard from women about their friends. Principles emerged from these stories that we found were working between us, and these became the basic building blocks of friendship in our book.

Our book could be much longer. After all, our lives are made up of stories—short, long, and in between—with neat or messy endings or with no ending. Everyone loves the chance to tell stories about her life. Good friends do this with one another. They show their caring by listening and by sharing. Stories have the potential to teach, inspire, or illustrate something. We then incorporate the experience told in the story with our own experiences. A story may resonate so much it leads us to modify future behavior.

Each story I heard changed me in some way, subtly or dramatically. Linda and I discussed them all and saw how they fit in with our friendship and other friendships. The book kept us open—with each other and with ourselves. Stumbles between us have been recognized and processed so quickly that they barely deserve mention. And yet I acknowledge that, in prior friendships, I might not have been so direct. Because of our work on the book, I believe I got braver with Linda more quickly. I had a hunch that our writing the book together would give me a unique opportunity to build a friendship consciously and well. We may not be long on experiences with each other, but we processed lifetimes of women's experiences with friendships, and I am grateful to each and every woman who told us her story.

I would, of course, like the book to make a difference in our readers' lives, just as I want to make a difference in my friends' lives and for them to make a difference in mine. One of my life's goals is to be an ever better friend. Writing this book has helped me, and perhaps readers will find themselves being better friends, too.

—MK

About the Authors

LINDA BUCKLIN, a wife and the mother of three sons, has worked in public relations and as a freelance writer. Honorary trustee of The Magic Theatre and Vice Regent of the Kenmore Museum, Fredericksburg, VA, she also serves as a Trustee for Grace Cathedral. Her other passions include hunting, camping, and fly-fishing in Montana; and competitive tennis. For the last ten years, she has been nationally ranked in women's senior tennis.

~

MARY KEIL lives in San Francisco with her husband and teenage son. She has been a banker, entrepreneur, and consultant. She produced the Broadway musical *Starmites*, for which she was nominated for a Tony Award for Best Musical. She produced the feature film *Angel Blue* and co-authored *Enterprise in the Nonprofit Sector*. Having lived in various parts of the country, she has a wide network of friendships.